American Water Tears:

A Grandmaster's Story

Han D. Cho

For My Mother

CONTENTS

ACKNOWLEDGMENT

My bro, my best man, always;

My sis, the super trooper;

My family, my life, especially Alice, for editing and for her support;

Randy Yu, for editing and for our lasting friendship;

My martial arts community, for believing in me – find your happiness with strength.

CHAPTER ONE
the news

When the red Camaro rolled onto Steve's driveway, he had to stare at it for a moment. It looked familiar, but he couldn't quite remember whom it belonged to. Certainly, it couldn't be his parents' friends', he thought. They wouldn't own a cramped up Camaro as a family vehicle. Many of them dropped by this time of the week – Fridays, after work. Steve wouldn't be able to see the driver since the guest would probably be using the back entrance to the house.

Despite the nagging curiosity, Steve decided to resume his bush trimming. But not for long. His feelings took over. There was something about the way the vehicle had rolled down his driveway – with a sort of trepidation. He needed to check it out. As he took his first step towards the garage, however, he heard the phone ring inside the house. His heart sank, and his mind took a sharp turn to something else. Who was it this time? What did they want now? He sure hoped that it wasn't Grandmother Wong. She would call at this time of the day. She knew his family's schedule well and wouldn't think twice about infringing on their personal time.

Someone picked up the phone. Steve felt relieved, at least temporarily. He couldn't take another series of dreadful phone rings today. He had way too much of that lately. His relief was soon replaced by fear with the sudden realization that perhaps his mother, Jasmine, had picked up the phone. Kimberly, his sister, opened the screen door and handed him the phone.

"I think you should answer this," said Kimberly. "Also, I have some mail for you. It's from your college. Should I bring it out to you?"

Kimberly seemed clueless about the problems the family was in. All the better, Steve thought. At least someone is enjoying life. Any sign of normalcy in the house was a good thing.

"Ahhhhh, does it look important?" Steve asked, going along with the normalcy.

"I don't know. I think so."

"Yeah, bring them."

"You mean bring *it*."

"Whatever." Steve rolled his eyes and managed a meager smile. He always found a little pleasure in the good people who tried to fix his grammar.

Kimberly went back in. Steve answered the phone.

"Hello."

"May I speak to Jasmine Lee?"

"Uh, who is this?"

"May I speak to Jasmine Lee?"

What? No 'please', Steve thought. These people were getting way too predictable.

"She does not speak English very well, so I'll speak on her behalf."

"Who is this?"

"I'm her son."

"What's your name?"

"What's your name? Who is this?" Steve knew who it was and what it was about as soon as he heard "May I speak to Jasmine Lee" but he played dumb. This was his small way of getting back at them, to play their own stupid game. It had become routine for him.

"This is the National Collection Agency. We are calling on behalf of the outstanding balance of twenty thousand one hundred twenty-three dollars and nineteen cents Jasmine Lee incurred using the XXXOOOO credit card. Our rec...."

"I thought I talked to you guys yesterday about that."

"Excuse me?"

"I talked to you guys yesterday."

"We have no record of your conversation with us yesterday. All our phone calls are closely monitored for...."

"No, I am positive. I talked to someone from your company

yesterday."

Steve continued to play dumb, interrupting just at the right moment.

"Could you wait for a moment? Let me check on that. Sometimes our different U.S. offices operate independently," said the man on the other line. Two things were clear about these collection agencies: they always had their male representatives call and they always made the company sound bigger than it really was.

"Listen, my name is Steve Lee. I am Jasmine Lee's son. Since she can't speak English, I handle all her affairs. Concerning your matter, I talked to somebody over there yesterday about the whole thing. We must've talked for more than an hour. He called my house at about 10:30 at night. I was ready to go to bed." Steve did what he could to elicit some sympathy from the faceless bully.

"Oh yes, here it is, it's coming up on the computer screen. It says here you did talk to one of our representatives yesterday, but I have no record of how you've resolved the matter with us."

"What do you mean? We must've talked for an hour. I explained every detail of our situation."

"Well, Sir, you have to explain it to me again." Steve felt that he had won a small battle after hearing 'sir' from the other side, but it didn't alleviate his growing frustration.

"This is the third time this week you guys called me for this, and I'm tired of explaining. Don't you have some kind of internal network to share your records?"

"Yes, we do, but sometimes our computers aren't updated by the time we make the next round of calls."

"I thought you said you monitored every call very closely."

"We do, Sir, and I'll make sure our conversation is documented as accurately as possible. But we need to talk about your account again."

Steve didn't buy that. They wanted him to explain, again and again until he gave in. They wanted money, not explanation. But two could play that game. The longer they talked, the more they would lose. After all, somebody had to pay for the stupid call.

"Look, I've told you time and time again, my mother didn't use the card, nor did she apply for the card or receive a bill. You guys made a huge mistake."

"My record indicates that Jasmine Lee resides in 1776 East Leslo Drive, Rudbury, Massachusetts. Is that correct?"

"Yes."

"And her social security number is 000-75-0123. Is that correct?"

"Yes, but...."

"And her birthday is June 5, 1944, is that correct?"

"Yes, but...."

"And her maiden name is Choi. Is that correct?"

"Yes. That is correct."

"Well then, we have all the records here, and it appears that we have the right person."

Steve was now fully frustrated. Though he faced the same approach twenty times before, his blood still boiled each time. His frustration wasn't even about the calls. It was about something else.

"Yes, but you have the wrong person. She never used, applied, nor received anything from you. If you want proof, then send somebody here. We'll prove it."

"You mean to tell me that she never used her card, and she never received monthly statements from us?"

"Yes, that's what I've been trying to tell your company. You've got the wrong person."

"All the purchases have her signatures on them. 'Jasmine Lee', they spell out."

"Well, they are not from her."

"None of them?"

"Yes, none of them."

"Sir, we find that hard to believe."

"Well then send somebody here right away. We'll prove it to you. My mother pays all her bills on time. She has never been late for anything. You can look at her records. If she had used your credit card, she would've paid it. In fact she has a credit card from another company with a perfectly good record. Call them. You want the number?"

Steve was getting more confident by the minute. At least this caller didn't try to interrupt him. Not that it mattered. By now, he knew all the angles.

"If Jasmine Lee didn't use the account, then who could've possibly used it? Would you have any idea?"

A shot of nerves ran through Steve's spine. He barely managed to utter the next words in a nonchalant manner.

"I don't know who used it. But that's not our concern is it?"

"Well, Sir, if Jasmine Lee didn't use the account, we would certainly like to know who did. Someone owes us a lot of money."

Money. The collection companies were the only ones who got to the point of the matter bluntly. Everyone else used the terms, "fee," "outstanding balance," "installment," to request money. Steve knew he should be glad for the company's directness with him, but not at this point.

"Like I said, I don't know. What I do know is that you guys have the wrong person. If you want proof, then send somebody here. I'll gladly provide whatever verification you want."

"Hmmmm...." The voice turned more compassionate. "Well, we could send you some documents for verification if you will cooperate. But I find it quite difficult to believe that she never received any monthly bills. Our record indicates that we've sent one every month for four months. In fact, the company had called about her lack of payment and sent extra letters to you before turning over the account to us."

"Yes, well, all we have to do is verify that, right? I'm telling you I'll cooperate. You guys can even bring somebody down today. We can have a face-to-face conversation. My mother couldn't have read your letter nor talked to you guys because she can't speak English. There was no way she could fill out one of your applications to get the card. As God is my witness, she had nothing to do with the account."

"Then who did?"

Again, a pang of pain. Steve felt exposed, as if the caller knew all along what Steve had tried to hide. "I don't know."

"Uh, huh." A long pause. "Well, I'll leave a record of our conversation with the manager, and send you some documents for verification. Could you send them back right way?"

"Yes I will. You can bet on it. If that's the only way to get you guys off my back, I'll do anything."

"Thank you, and have a good day," and he hung up.

Steve felt relief. This one was nicer. Though he knew by now the problem would never end and the phone calls would continue to mount, he still felt some sense of accomplishment at making someone on the other side understand, even if it came down to nothing. The computer would recycle Jasmine's number again and the phone calls would start again, but at least he felt safe for the rest of the day. Sooner or later, they had to stop. Although by then, Steve would've probably talked to everyone in the whole company, even if none of them ever updated their freakin' computers.

Kimberly brought out Steve's mail. Steve handed the phone back to her and quickly glanced at all three letters, but none was what he was looking for. None from Jane. He wondered if she would ever write back. Again, he felt that sinking feeling.

"I'm going to the grocery store. Want anything?" said Kimberly, sensing Steve's gloomy mood to which she had become accustomed after these calls. Her easygoing demeanor calmed him.

"No. How do you like the car so far?"

"It's okay."

"Well, we'll buy you a better one next time. It's all we could afford right now. Hey, at least it's red, the color you wanted."

Kimberly smiled a little. She was a good sport.

"For your information, Mister, it's not red, it's maroon. But it's okay. I like it. It'll do."

"At least the brakes work really well. Mom and I were sold on that. Also, it has front-wheel drive so you'll have no problem in the snow. The route you need to take for your college is all highways, you know. Remember to pump your brakes." Steve was doing what he could to convince himself that the family's decision to get her an old Ford Escort for her long commute to college was the best they could do. "Also, Escorts are reliable, so you won't have to worry about it breaking down in the middle of the highway."

"I told you, it's fine."

Kimberly's passive acceptance didn't help Steve's increasing guilt.

"We'll get you a better car in the future. I promise."

"See you," said Kimberly. As Steve watched her walk away he wondered if she was going to see her on-again, off-again boyfriend who was working at the K-mart next to the grocery store she was supposed to go to. Probably. Why else would she want to go to the grocery store without Mom? She had her makeup on and wrapped herself with tight denim shorts and a baby Tee. Steve wanted to say something to her but didn't. Some things cannot be learned by the head.

Steve opened his letters. All of them were from the college where he recently graduated. One was a receipt of the promissory note for his student loan payment. The other was from the Alumni Office asking for a contribution. The last one was from the Asian-American Coalition Group asking for his participation in the area – money, of course. Whether it was "involvement," "memories of yesteryear," "opinion," or "bonding events," it was always about the money.

Steve folded the letters and stuffed them in his back pockets. They were the kind of letters he couldn't throw away but didn't want to keep. They would usually linger in his pockets until he would empty them onto his tabletop, where they would accumulate into a massive pile. The pile would then be stuffed into a desk drawer, where it would sit for centuries until he realized that they were junk in the first place, at which point he would toss them away. Still, he thought, if he had the money, it would be fun to give a large donation to the Alumni Office, and maybe have his name carved on one of the doors of his engineering school buildings, or to be the President of the Asian Coalition and mingle with professional Asians, traveling and impressing people, girls especially, as most guys want to do. So he kept the letters, temporarily, to motivate himself. Or maybe he kept them because he wanted souvenirs of his college years that had gone by too fast.

Steve grabbed his hedge shears again and headed off to trim the last bush, located on the left edge of the front yard. As he rounded the corner, he noticed the red Camaro parked away from the garage with its engine still running, the windows glaring in the August sun. He had momentarily forgotten about the vehicle. Gripping his hedge shears tighter, Steve walked over.

Just as he got close enough to touch the driver-side door, the window rolled down. The glaring tinted window was slowly replaced by a familiar face. It was Benny, the best friend of Steve's brother, Charlie. Steve remembered then whom the vehicle belonged to. It couldn't have belonged to anyone else. Actually, the same thing happened the last time Steve saw Benny's vehicle. He could never remember Benny's vehicle until he saw Benny in it, and then the vehicle familiarized itself like an old friend.

"Hey, Steve, what's up, mang?"

Steve was reminded of Benny's subtle Cuban accent. A sense of bittersweetness came over him, more bitter than sweet.

"Hey. What's up, Benny? Why aren't you coming in?"

"Oh, it's too hot outside, mang. I just wanted get some air-conditioning."

"Shit, I don't blame you. It's hot out."

"Been doing some trimming, I see."

"Yeah."

Despite many lingering questions, Steve decided to remain patient. He had been known to overreact to Charlie's mishaps in front of Benny many times before, so he wanted to stay cool this time, especially since Charlie wasn't around.

"Charlie's not here," Steve said, anticipating the reason for Benny's visit.

"I know," Benny said, as he shut his engine off and got out the vehicle.

Steve's heart plunged.

Benny's six-foot height and large shoulders swelled out of the tiny interior. He wore jean shorts and a white tee shirt with inscriptions of some rock band Steve couldn't identify. His white socks didn't match his brown boat shoes. His skin was pale even at this time of the summer. There was a roll of fat underneath his neatly tucked shirt, something Steve hadn't seen on him before.

"It's been a long time," Steve said.

"Yeah. Your brother told me you'd be home this summer."

"You know where he is then?"

"No, I haven't seen him recently."

"I see. Shit, where the Hell is he?" Steve spoke to himself.

"Listen, Steve, mang. I gotta talk to you."

"Yeah, sure. What's up?"

Benny looked around to see if anyone was there, making Steve even more nervous. Steve knew it had something to do with Charlie. They walked towards the house, and found a shaded spot. It wasn't any cooler. There was no escaping the humid air. Steve wondered why they had to be in the shade anyway. Did Benny think that he was going to say something that was so shocking that Steve would collapse under the hot sun?

"You know, Charlie's not doing well, mang."

"I know."

"The last time I saw him...."

Steve looked up at Benny. "Yeah?"

Benny paused for a moment. Then he spoke in a voice that made Steve believe him instantly. There was no denial stage on this one, not at all.

"Yo, mang, he's on drugs. He's doing too much of that stuff."

Drugs!

Steve's knees buckled. He let go of the hedge shears, backtracked a few steps and crumpled down on the pathway stairs, the rest of his body sagging like a bag of rice.

The fact that Benny was the one who came with the news didn't make things any easier. Although he had known Benny for about seven years now, they hardly ever exchanged words other than proper greetings or short chats to acknowledge their co-existence. In fact, this was the first time they actually conversed beyond the normal pleasantries. Without Charlie, they would've never bothered to know each other.

But now Benny was here in front of Steve, pleading his friend's case, Charlie's case, speaking directly to Steve, with Charlie nowhere in sight. It must be bad, Steve could only imagine. He gathered his composure, tilted his head up towards Benny and, fighting the bright sun, asked how bad Charlie was into it, mildly surprised by the serenity of his own voice. Was the tone appropriately reflecting his shocked state, or was it a subconscious revelation of the lack of care and concern he now had for Charlie?

Benny didn't reply, however, returning only a sullen stare, the darkness of his countenance enhanced by the contrast of the bright sun behind him.

There couldn't have been any worse way to answer. The world became even more bleak for Steve. Just when he thought the well had run dry on bad things happening to him, just when he thought he had hit rock bottom, Benny delivered the final blow, the knockout punch Steve had been ducking all year long. It was the beginning of the end. For real.

CHAPTER TWO
the separation

Steve and Charlie spent their childhood in the busy streets of Korea. From the very beginning, Charlie was restless. He never stopped crying as a baby and never stopped moving as a toddler. As a child, Charlie was the most adventurous among his peers, and therefore, the most popular. He didn't consciously try to attract attention, things just happened to him naturally; trouble always found Charlie. When Charlie wanted something, he got it. Being the firstborn, Charlie was too easily forgiven by Jasmine and his father, Jang, who rarely discouraged his boundless behavior. Jasmine and Jang didn't have much, but they would've preferred to be in deep debt than to deprive their firstborn son of his irreplaceable childhood experiences, especially because they never had them. They wanted Charlie to have normal childhood experiences like everyone else. The problem was that Charlie never was a normal child.

Whenever there was a fight in town among kids, Charlie was involved. Many kids frequently challenged Charlie because of his immense popularity. Charlie gambled a lot, too. Whether with marbles, trading cards, or money, Charlie's games were always big enough to cause a scene; kids on the block dropped whatever they were doing just to sneak a peek at his big ego in action. Wherever Charlie went, there were always mobs of kids who followed him. He was always in the thick of the action because he was the action. He could mobilize an army of kids in a heartbeat whenever he wanted to play a game or scheme a trick. He never wanted the attention, but the kids just didn't leave him alone. Charlie was their rebel-without-a-cause leader.

Once, after watching a Tarzan movie with a group of kids, Charlie climbed a tall tree and cleverly swung himself across from one side of the tree to the other side using a hanging rope.

"Ahh..ahhh…ahh..ahhh!" Charlie screamed, just like Tarzan. The kids looked at him in awe. The incident caused a new trend in the neighborhood and many broken limbs from the poor saps who did their best to imitate him. The hyped stories of injuries were told like war wounds, which only fueled more kids to try swinging wilder. When exasperated parents of the injured and injured-to-be couldn't prevent their kids from playing Tarzan, they decided to chop the old tree down. In fact, quite a few more trees were chopped down thereafter.

Then Charlie became interested in fire. After watching a popular TV cartoon series where they shot fire beams from spaceships, Charlie managed to throw a giant firebomb, made from a crude metal bucket filled with the residue of hot coals, that spectacularly streaked across the night sky before exploding onto the ground with the bright sparks of fireworks. Nights were never the same after that. Kids of all ages started to compete to find out who could outdo Charlie's legendary firebomb. Ignoring their curfews, ignoring their lack of knowledge of trajectory, kids set off firebombs in the night sky where the moon was the only other source of light. Startled adults had to form a coalition to outlaw the firebombs. The firebombs burned houses, trees, barns, dogs, cats, and, yes, the kids. The Adult Coalition Against Firebomb-Throwing Kids meeting was said to have taken place in the tiny waiting room of the town's only hospital while the doctors and nurses treated the burnt faces and limbs of confused children who were busy wondering why the comic heroes in TV had never gotten burned themselves.

Then Charlie entered his hobo-admiring stage and his glorification of being free and independent. Among the escapades he concocted to live this newly acclaimed life of his, he was particularly fond of one – to eat only what he had killed. Enter his slingshot phase – for hunting, of course. When the neighborhood kids watched him shoot down a little bird from fifty feet away with a stone launched from the crude slingshot he had carved himself, Charlie started another trend – this time a trend of dangerous epic proportion.

Immediately, all the available slingshots in stores within the three neighboring towns were gone. So were the birds. With no birds to hunt, Charlie got bored and schemed a war game where the kids could shoot each other. And the war game spread like a wildfire in a monsoon wind. Within days, hundreds of kids from all over the town and the neighboring cities were shooting stones at each other.

Random stones flew in all direction. Windows were smashed, houses damaged, and many Hangari (clay pots people used to store food) were destroyed. No one was safe. Most of the younger kids, including Steve, couldn't even go outside or stay near the paper screen doors. Babies, children, adults, and grandparents were sent to the hospital – blood flowing down their heads, eyes, arms and legs. This time the town officials, including the Mayor and the Police Chief, stepped in. So did the weekly news.

There was a time when Steve envied Charlie. Steve wanted to be like his older brother who was the king of the neighborhood. He didn't even mind getting in trouble with him just to be with him. But, that all changed after one fateful day.

Charlie had stolen a considerable sum of money from home, hid it in a bush and planned to trick Steve into thinking that they found the money. After placing the money in a plastic bag with valuable toys – some high-tech assemble-it-yourself model planes, bubble gum, expensive American-made chewing gum (even the wrappers on this gum were high in value among the kids who traded them, vigorously) – and then hiding the bag in a bush near the hill where they lived, Charlie hastily dragged Steve out in the middle of his nap for a let's-bond-as-brothers walk, the first of its kind. Of course, Steve was too young and naive to suspect how Charlie could've seen from an impossible angle a plastic bag loaded with an unimaginable amount of treasure hidden deep in a bush. Adventures certainly found Charlie! Steve was thrilled at their discovery and immediately imagined how happy Jasmine would be. He happened to know that she was in dire need of some fast cash. Something about Jang needing to travel. The timing was perfect, Steve had thought, as if God had sent it to him! There wasn't even a name or address to return the goodies to the rightful owner.

But before Steve could say anything, Charlie urged him to keep their find a secret. Then he bought Steve all kinds of goodies, like popular comic books, assemble-it-yourself toys, more bubble gum, and even a bottle of genuine Coca Cola – a genuine Coca Cola! The pop culture of America! America itself! Though Steve had heard about it, he never dreamt that he would ever have a chance to taste one! – a whole bottle of it at that! All Steve could do was hold the bottle in his hand, dumbstruck. Charlie had downed his in one long gulp, but Steve couldn't even sip his, still shocked to have the elixir of life in his hand. Ahhhhh...success! It really was exciting to be with Charlie – The Adventure of Treasure Island.

As the day went by, however, Steve soon suspected foul play. That night, Jasmine was lamenting over some missing money, which seemed to roughly equal the amount that Charlie and Steve had found. When Steve tried to tell her about their find, Charlie quickly covered Steve's mouth and dragged him out of their one-room apartment. Steve didn't suspect anything even after that, but Charlie's persistence to keep him quiet finally did.

Steve was in turmoil. It was a unique kind of problem, something he had never dealt with before. This problem had no clear solution. If he confessed to Jasmine, then he and Charlie would be sure to receive some major punishment, especially Charlie. And snitching was such a weaselly thing to do. Charlie would probably never include him in anything else ever again. On the other hand, not telling meant that he was exploiting Jasmine. Only the worst crook in the world would steal from his mother. Silence seemed to be the easiest solution because nobody would get hurt. Jasmine would be able to live with the idea that there was a burglary in the house better than with the idea that her sons had stolen money from her. All Steve had to do was keep his mouth shut.

Steve tried to convince Charlie not to spend any more of the money, but the pleas only increased Charlie's generosity towards him. Steve didn't enjoy Charlie's attention anymore. The problem was too big for him to bear. He had never imagined that he would be stealing his mother's money, especially when she seemed to struggle so much with it, or from the lack of it. Steve couldn't live with that, anything but that. Still, Steve maintained his silence, if only due to Charlie's solemn pleas.

By week's end, however, Steve decided to confess. He had had enough. Charlie did his best to stop him and even offered him the rest of the money, but this time his pleas only fueled Steve's decision even more. Defeated, Charlie ran away and hid himself on the hill, monitoring Steve's moves as he reached Jasmine, who was washing clothes in the town's public water station. She was holding a large stick that women used to beat the clothes. While she repeatedly hit the laundry with the stick, Steve flinched in sheer terror, knowing the impending fate that lay before him. He could hardly breathe.

"Uhhh...Mommy?"

"What is it, Dear?" she answered without looking.

"I...I have to tel..."

"Honey, I'm busy right now. I have to get these clothes washed before the sunset. Could you play with your friends in the meantime?"

Steve stood still, not knowing what else to do. Jasmine continued to beat her laundry. After rinsing one of the shirts and fetching another one from the bucket, she noticed Steve again.

"Honey? What's the matter? Are you okay?"

"I have to tell you something."

This time, the other women around her looked up. Many of them washed clothes, some washed rice for supper, and some cleaned dishes. It was a busy time for the only water pump on the block.

Jasmine stopped and gave Steve her full attention.

"What is it, Dear?"

"Mommy, I have to tell you something."

"Okay, go ahead."

Steve hardly made any sense, murmuring his confession, and she had a difficult time comprehending his reluctant dribbles, but when she finally did, he felt like he was experiencing the Korean War himself. It certainly didn't help that she was embarrassed by her neighborhood friends, tsk-tsking their lips and shaking their heads as they watched Steve being violently dragged away to a firing squad.

That day, Charlie and Steve received one of the most memorable punishments of their lives. The whips had broken into many pieces by the time Jasmine was done with Charlie, leaving him with shiny red marks all over his legs, arms, and back. After the whips had been rendered ineffective, she used the large flyswatter until it broke in three, prompting frequent trips to the hill to find different sized tree branches. Charlie must've thanked God a hundred times that the big tree had been chopped down during his Tarzan phase. Otherwise, she would've had an unlimited source of whips, and the punishment might've never ended.

The scariest part of the punishment for Steve wasn't the punishment itself, but the tense moments before his actual punishment; they seemed to last forever, especially when he could see Charlie's wretched, contorted face. Jasmine usually punished Charlie first because he was older and probably the guiltier of the two. And Steve was always next, even when he wasn't guilty of anything. Jasmine told Steve many years later that she had punished Charlie and him together to give them the sense of bond between them, good or bad, because they should always be responsible for each other.

After Jasmine was done with Charlie, she turned her inevitable attention to Steve. Luckily, Steve received his beating with a smaller, sort-of-emergency whip that she kept under a chest closet in case she ran out of every option. Jasmine was also too tired from all the energy spent on beating Charlie to hand out a proper beating to Steve. Nevertheless, the beating was memorable for him. He took it well. The pain neutralized the emotional turmoil he had endured before the confession. Steve noticed Jasmine crying as she lashed out her punishment. He had no idea that her anger wasn't due to the incident, but rather to the helpless feeling that an unfortunate twist in her life had resulted in her children committing such an act. All they wanted were toys to have some fun; something she couldn't provide. Each whip she lashed out cut through her heart tenfold deeper.

Jasmine's tears that day stayed with Steve. From that day, Charlie and Steve went their separate ways. Though they remained close and loved and protected each other fiercely, they realized that they were different from each other. Steve chose the conventional path, and Charlie continued to choose shortcuts. Even when Steve was young, knowing which path was the correct path was easy for him. All he had to do was learn from Charlie's follies.

CHAPTER THREE
charlie's follies

In truth, Steve had sensed the possibility that Charlie might be involved with drugs. How could he not? With all those lost souls Charlie hung out with in Ashton, it was only a matter of time. Against his better judgment, however, Steve had decided to ignore the possibility. It wasn't like he could do anything about it. He couldn't very well accuse Charlie without any proof either. Charlie wasn't a kid anymore, and this wasn't a kid's game. There had to be a point when a person took responsibility for his own actions.

The main reason for Steve's suspicion were Charlie's unusually violent mood swings. But then, Charlie always had a quick temper. It didn't take drugs to make Charlie erratic; one moment he would be the best friend in the world and the next moment he would be angry enough to gouge out your soul and eat it. The year of the dragons – Charlie was born in the Spring of 1964 – were famous for that kind of temperament, so the saying goes in Korea.

In any case, Steve didn't have the luxury of dealing with more problems; there were enough of them already. Charlie had created a major disaster for the family through his insurance business scam. The victims of his scam wanted retribution from Steve's family since most of the customers in the business were through the network of family friends. Kimberly was going through rough times with a boy who wasn't treating her well, and Steve himself was going through a breakup. On top of all that, the family was on the verge of bankruptcy: Jasmine, the main breadwinner of the family, was no longer able to work due to a career-ending back injury at the factory. The Lee family was in crisis, financially, emotionally, physically, and psychologically.

Charlie was recruited by Mr. Poe, who wanted an heir to take over his auto insurance business, which mainly served the Korean community in the area. The business wasn't highly profitable, but it had a solid foundation because of its loyal clienteles. The number of Koreans in the community was growing rapidly and service industries like Mr. Poe's insurance business were beginning to be high in demand. Steve's family was one of Mr. Poe's loyal clients.

On a casual encounter with Jasmine and Jang, Mr. Poe, who was close to retirement age, had expressed that he wanted a successor to carry on his business. Jasmine and Jang, eager to help their son find a career, had suggested Charlie to Mr. Poe. In no time at all, from among other prospective applicants, Mr. Poe decided on Charlie. Charlie appeared to be the perfect candidate: smart, witty, and proficient in both Korean and English.

At first, Charlie wasn't receptive to the idea. But then, it wasn't in his nature to accept other people's suggestions without making a fuss about it. Eventually, after some encouragements from Jasmine and Jang, Charlie obliged and even appeared excited. Of course, Jasmine and Jang were more relieved than glad to have finally found a spot in society where Charlie could settle. Charlie's new career as an insurance man had potential and was fairly risk-free. Certainly, it wasn't a bad way to make a living and earn respect at the same time, or so they had thought.

Charlie wanted to succeed in his new career and quickly. He wanted to obtain all the necessary permits and licenses. Jasmine was more than willing to fund whatever Charlie requested. In addition to the insurance business, Charlie wanted to tap into the real estate market. He figured those who owned a vehicle would eventually want to buy a house or business properties. The Koreans were ambitious people. Owning a beautiful house was at the top of their priority list, because such was the unanimously assumed mark of success.

It was a great idea, typical of Charlie: smart, keen, and opportunistic. He always looked for an angle that others missed, including Mr. Poe, even with his thirty years of experience. But the plan also showed another typical side of Charlie: the one that liked to leap before learning to walk. Charlie hadn't even begun his new career as an insurance agent, and yet he already acted like a veteran. Enticed by the lure of easy money, Charlie embezzled the company's revenue soon after he settled into his position. He never had any intention to steal it; he only wanted to borrow it for a short while so that he could pay off the mounting debts from his frivolous spending. He had planned on replacing it before anybody knew it was gone. Charlie didn't have a bad heart, just a weak soul. He never sought thrills from the troubles he caused, he simply didn't think through the consequences thoroughly. It was always easy for him to hide his face in a hole and let others around him fix his mistakes. He had a heart of gold, but the courage of a goldfish. He could never be a devil himself, though he could always be sold to one. Eventually, some unfortunate clients who were involved in vehicle accidents realized their vehicles weren't insured properly, and all Hell broke loose.

The outraged clients phoned Jasmine and Jang constantly. It is natural in any culture to link a child's behavior to that of his/her parents, but the parent-child connection goes beyond reasonable in Korean culture. Unable to locate Charlie, who by now was disappearing from the family as well, Jasmine tried vainly to negotiate the customers' demands for reparation of the damages to their vehicles, the amount of which increased rather mysteriously each time they spoke. This was particularly true of one of the clients, whom everyone called Grandmother Wong. She was representing her son, a friend of Jasmine and Jang, whose six-year-old, pre-owned Honda Civic was stolen. Grandmother Wong had survived World War II and the Korean War, and she tackled her claim like a survivor.

Grandmother Wong called every day. Each time she called she raised the cost of the damage by remembering different valuable items left in the vehicle that her son had forgotten to mention, such as the brand new state-of-the art Bose sound system, the Rolex watch, the diamond ring, and, of course, the wallet with five hundred dollars of cash in it. When Jasmine tried to question Grandmother Wong's translucent lies, the old lady would have fits and threaten to call the police, but not before threatening Charlie's life and cursing Jasmine's generation to Hell. Jasmine promised her the full cost of the vehicle, but Grandmother Wong's demands mounted high enough to buy a brand new one.

Steve was outraged. His American senses told him to argue – that by law his family wasn't responsible for Charlie's actions, that the damages couldn't be more than the total cost of the vehicle less the scrap value, that the insurance didn't cover personal belongings, that Grandmother Wong shouldn't threaten the life of her son's insurance agent and his family every day, and that she herself didn't have any right to make claims about the accident because it wasn't her policy. Steve was particularly angry at Grandmother Wong's son, the owner of the vehicle, the so-called family friend, who mysteriously disappeared during the process.

But Steve's Korean senses kept him quiet. It was rude to argue with elders.

The phone calls weren't limited to Charlie's insurance follies. Charlie had many unpaid credit card bills. He forged different credit card accounts under Jasmine's name and defaulted on the payments after racking up huge bills. Eventually, these accounts were turned over to collection agencies. Because of Jasmine's lack of English, Steve had to answer their calls. He tried desperately to let the companies know that she had never applied, received, nor used their credit cards. It was tricky for him to do this without giving away any information about Charlie's involvement. However, the collection companies weren't going to let him off that easily. As soon as Steve had spent hours finally convincing one agent, the collection company's computer would reset Jasmine's phone number and issue another harassment call by a different agent who would end up asking the same question: where was the money? Sometimes they would try the nice approach and listen to Steve's elaborate explanations, but other times they were more personal and downright condescending, as in you-have-no-right-to-be-here-in-my-country-causing-trouble-for-a-good-ol'-American-like-me attitude. Steve did his best to maintain his composure with them, but as the summer wore on and the phone calls continued, he couldn't help but have enormous shouting matches with them.

The phone calls didn't stop there. Charlie also reneged on his vehicle payments. It wasn't just any vehicle, but a brand new convertible Corvette which was, of course, under Jasmine's name. Funny how these creditors could lend their goods so easily but were so unforgiving when it came to collecting their debts, especially when all they had to do was select their clients more carefully in the beginning. In the boom days of the late 80s, everyone was swept away by the bubble economy. Jasmine tried her best to make the payments, but eventually the vehicle was repossessed. The phone calls from the dealer about the details of the Corvette's outstanding balance and the cost of repossession didn't stop, however.

There was no doubt in Steve's mind that tales of Charlie's follies would soon circulate among the Korean community and become the hot topic of their daily gossip. Though the Korean community was spaced out over different towns, it was nonetheless a tight community. They stayed connected through friends, casual encounters, and formal gatherings: Korean grocery stores, parties, cookouts, church activities, Gyes (informal loaning among a group of people), political functions, and even Veteran association meetings. Learning, evolving, and assimilating into the American culture, the Koreans supported each other to cope with life on foreign soil, and also competed with each other to see who could be more successful in capturing that American Dream. *'Did you hear what happened with the Lee family and what Charlie did? He took his clients' money and ran and did drugs with it! Can you imagine the nerve of him? And here we thought the Lee's knew how to raise their children. How shameful!'* Sometimes, the measure of success was more evident if compared with failure.

The phone calls went on during most of the day and into odd hours of the night or early morning. With each ring, Steve could envision an angry old lady wanting more money and cursing his family to Hell once again, or an ignorant employee from the collection agency harassing for repayments, or unsympathetic lawyers, representing the Corvette dealer, with their sophisticated litigation lingo intended to intimidate the family into payment, or the thugs at the junkyard responsible for repossessing the Corvette looking to break some bones for their unpaid services, or more news of Charlie's follies in his down-and-out condition.

Because of her sense of responsibility, especially to the complaining Koreans, Jasmine didn't want to unhook the phone. Sometimes, however, both Steve and Jasmine would be so frustrated with the calls that they would leave the phones ringing.

Ringgggggggggg.... ringgggggggg... ringgggggggggg.... ringgggggggg..... ringgggggggg... ringgggggggg....

The dreadful sound bounced off the walls, the floors, and the ceilings, cutting the gloomy silence that enveloped their house and shook the very foundation of their dignity and self-worth, reminding them how unforgiving and hostile the outside world can be, and how hopelessly lost they were. Most of all, Steve feared the effects these calls had on Jasmine. The calls bothered him because they bothered her. They were sounds of her failures, despite all her efforts. Jasmine was on the edge of her sanity. In the heat of the summer of '89, the Lee family's house was filled with strange and suffocating energy: the feeling of chaos, the feeling of craziness, the feeling of doom. And Charlie was nowhere in sight.

CHAPTER FOUR
get charlie

Benny and Charlie became friends during their high school days. They hung out so often that Charlie even started to pick up some Cuban accents and slangs, like adding "mang" to every sentence. *'Hey, mang, what's up?* Benny was sort of big, sort of good-looking, sort of smart, sort of ambitious, sort of nice, sort of athletic, sort of popular. Nothing about him stood out except the words "sort of." On the other hand, Charlie throughout his life was anything but "sort of." Of all Charlie's friends, Steve liked Benny the most. Benny was normal. Others talked a lot. Charlie was always generous to his friends. Too generous. One of the charges on the credit card Charlie had used before forfeiting his payment was for ten microwave ovens – ten freakin' microwave ovens! Steve was sure that Benny was the only one who wouldn't take such a handout from Charlie.

Benny patiently waited for Steve to say something, but Steve didn't know what to say. He didn't know how to resolve this crisis that was all too common a theme on the many TV shows he had watched. The drug news in the 80's made headlines almost daily. President Reagan had even declared America a War on Drugs. Everyone was captivated by this new wave of devastating culture that swept the country. In fact, Steve prided himself on being some sort of expert from watching all those shows about drugs.

The camera rolls on a city street full of liquor bottles covered in brown paper bags and cigarette butts. The sound of hip-hop music starts. The voice of an angry rapper jams in celebration and condemnation of poverty and getting high. The camera spots a small junkie barely supporting her weight against a graffiti-filled wall. She blinks with strain, no hint of a glimmer in her eyes to be found. Then comes, ever so subtly, a slow-mo shot of two young men with coiled muscles making drug exchanges, moving so casually that you can tell they have done this a thousand times before. The camera zooms above the city, slowly taking in the full view of the poverty-stricken area while a narrator times it perfectly and blurts out, "...plagued by the mass destruction of lost dreams," the roaring beat of hip-hop stays long after the screen becomes dark.

The media's glamorous portrayal of drugs was a drug in itself. Now that Steve had the chance to feel what it was like, he was ashamed of his ignorance. Helplessness was what he felt the most. It was the one feeling Steve was getting tired of these days. He'd had enough.

Something stirred inside him, speeding his heart, heating his blood vessels. He knew it was time. He knew what he had to do. What he needed to do. He got up and went to the front door of the house.

"Mom, I'm gonna go out for a while. I'll try to bring Brother home with me," Steve said as he opened the door, aware of the absurdity of his announcement.

He didn't see Jasmine but he knew she was in the kitchen. He could hear the familiar sound of her cutting board. She never stayed still from cleaning, cooking, and rearranging. When she ran out of things to do, she would re-clean the clean things, making them sparkle more. The pots and pans shined so brightly that he always felt reluctant to use them. When she ran out of things to re-clean, she rearranged the furniture. There was no furniture too big or too heavy for her to move. Every day Steve would hear the familiar sound of dishes being washed, food being cooked, the sound of vacuums, the sound of sweeping and mopping, the sound of the washing machine, and the sound of everything in the house being rearranged. He even developed a habit of letting these sounds rock him to sleep.

"What are you talking about?" asked Jasmine.

"I'm gonna try to bring Brother home."

"You don't even know where he is. How could you bring him home?" She replied, clearly surprised by Steve's announcement.

There was energy in her voice, however. That was all the encouragement Steve needed.

"I'm sure he's at the beach somewhere. I will head on over there."

"Maybe...."

Just then, Jang, who was eavesdropping from the living room, cut in.

"I'll go with you," he said enthusiastically, as if he had been waiting all day for his cue.

"Should I go, too?" Jasmine asked.

She seemed eager, her eyes widening. It was nice for Steve to see her so perked up, almost to a point of relief. It had been a while since she had done that.

"No, you stay. We'll go," Jang ordered, implying that this was a man's thing, and that she should stay put.

Instead of being annoyed at Jang's all too familiar attitude, Steve felt rather special this time. Yes, true, some things should be done by men. Besides, she was in no condition to go anywhere, certainly not on any freaky adventure. What would've happened if she saw her drugged-out, first-born son acting crazy? It was too risky.

"Yeah, Mom. Stay. You're too weak to go. We'll bring him here soon enough."

"OK. Be careful," she said, seeming to realize her physical

limitations.

Or maybe this time she wanted to support that Man's Way. She never hated the macho world she was brought up in; in fact, she embraced it. She was more than happy to play the good, courteous, wife role for the rest of her life, if only her husband knew how to bring home the bacon for the family.

"You should eat before you go. Everything is ready, and it'll take only a few minutes to heat up," said Jasmine.

"No, Mom. We'll bring him home before supper. It'll get dark if we eat now and then go look for him. I'm not really hungry anyway."

Steve was aware that his adrenaline was building. A full stomach would only bring complacency. Fear could help him if he channeled it correctly and hurt him if he didn't. He learned this in the martial arts that he practiced ever since he was a kid. On more than one occasion, he had used fear as a positive energy that gave him the winning edge in competitions. Now he needed that edge more than ever.

Steve went to his room to change. He put on khaki pants and a long-sleeved oxford shirt that used to be sky blue before Jasmine washed it to white. She washed all the laundry twice, prolonging the soaking time for extra cleanliness. Just about every piece of clothing in the house turned white over time. Though a long-sleeved shirt wasn't ideal for the hot sun, he opted for a more mature look. It would take maturity to convince Charlie to come home. He wondered if Jasmine knew that Charlie was involved with drugs. Maybe she suspected it, but didn't dare to admit it to herself. That was the problem with her. As strong-willed as she was, she lacked conviction where it counted the most, with her children. Especially Charlie. She loved him more than anyone else in the whole world and Charlie could walk all over her whenever he wanted.

As Steve stepped out the front door, Jasmine packed some fruit in a brown lunch bag and handed it to him. Steve wished she hadn't done that, but he made no fuss about it. Soldiers are supposed to be sent off with a salute and some manly words of encouragement like "Good luck, Men" or "God speed," not with a little picnic basket and worrisome eyes.

"You should've seen your brother last spring. You wouldn't have recognized him because he got so skinny. He's probably not eating from all the guilt. I want him to have a warm meal. I didn't tell you this, but I had a terrible dream the other night. I saw him floating lifelessly in a river. No matter what I did, I couldn't stop him from drifting downward. I need to see him. I need to see him with my own eyes."

In times of crisis, Jasmine talked about her dreams a lot. They foreshadowed her crises, which she wouldn't have dared to acknowledge during her waking hours. On more than one occasion, her dreams were uncannily accurate.

"Okay, Mom. Don't worry so much. Everything should be fine."

Jasmine's words strengthened Steve, and validated his decision to bring his drugged-out brother home, even if he had to carry him.

"Yeah. We'll bring him back," said Jang.

Again, Steve was caught off guard by how suddenly Jang entered into the whole picture. Still, he was more glad than annoyed. Jang would have a better chance of finding Charlie than Steve. On good days, Jang and Charlie were the best father and son team on the planet, laughing and backslapping each other about their many hunting, fishing, and gambling adventures. Seeing them get along so well together, Steve often wondered why they argued so much.

Benny wanted to follow Steve in his own vehicle. Steve found that a little strange but didn't ask. Maybe Benny wanted the option of bailing out if things got too rough. He didn't even have to go. By the time the three of them were on the road, it was around five o'clock in the afternoon and the sun still blazed over the western sky.

CHAPTER FIVE
bark at the moon

The Korean War was started on June 25, 1950 by Kim Il Sung, the leader of communist North Korea. His sole purpose was to invade the democratic nation of South Korea and launch a hostile takeover to unify the countries that had been divided for many years. During the three years of war, the momentum of the war shifted back and forth between the combined forces of the Communist regime from North Korea, and later China, and the combined forces of the democracy of South Korea, with the aid of the United Nations. As a result, the weary citizens of the war-torn land were forced to pledge their allegiance to one of the conflicting sides. Many lost their lives in the name of treason when the balance of power shifted back to the opposing side. People were insane and everyone blamed everyone else for the senseless deaths of their loved ones.

As the war neared its end, many civilians were killed by the retreating communists. They wanted to make an indelible mark before giving up their conquests. It was the most difficult time for the civilians to survive because everyone wanted to carry out his own means of justice and revenge before the killings became uncommon again. Violence does not end just because a war ends. There is always justice and revenge, and justice upon revenge, and revenge upon justice.

Steve's grandfather, Dong-Yang, was especially vulnerable to this dangerous and unstable social climate because he was the successful police chief of a small village in mid-western Korea called Youngdae. Being any part of the long-arm-of-the-law commanded high respect and carried an almost celebrity-like image, especially if you were the chief of police. Everyone respected him. The first thing the Communist regime did after invading the village was look for Dong-Yang. The Communist party didn't like intellectuals or any other elite members of society because they could potentially disrupt their system. The party wanted good followers, ones who didn't question authority. Most of the prominent members of the community, like teachers, politicians, police officers, community leaders, and religious leaders were arrested, tortured, raped and/or executed. Dong-Yang was already the Most Wanted Felon, and he was sure to be executed upon his capture. The search for Dong-Yang tightened even more as the Communist regime sensed the urgency to retreat from Youngdae, due to the successful retaliation mounted by General MacArthur and the U.N. forces.

Sensing the end of the war and unable to withstand his longing to see his family, particularly his two daughters, Dong-Yang foolishly came out of hiding and visited his home, and fell right into the hands of the vicious communist police force and communist-pledged villagers. They were staking out for him after a hot tip from a neighbor eager to please the new party. In the midst of meeting his daughter, Dong-Yang received a piercing bullet in his stomach, one in his chest, one in the shoulder, one in the back, one to the neck, another to the chest, and yet another to the back. Jasmine, the daughter who was eagerly waiting to be embraced by her father, saw the whole thing. Through her seven-year-old eyes, she saw her father fall to the ground in blood-soaked clothing, speaking to her for the last time.

"Jasmine...oh, Jasmine...I'm..so...s..o..r..r..y..."

He received seven shots, seven *precious* bullets. Most civilians were killed by suffocation or buried alive to save the *precious* bullets, but Dong-Yang, the chief of police, the elite of the elite – the man who wandered around for most of his life as a drifter until he fell in love with a woman fifteen years younger, the man who held his first baby at the late age of forty-two, the man who frequently left work early just to come home to hold his daughters – left the world with a family that consisted of a young, hapless wife, four-year-old and seven-year-old daughters, still in the midst of the war, with seven bullets in his body...apologizing.

Bang-Bang-Bang-Bang-Bang-Bang-Bang!

Just like that, Jasmine's security on life dropped from the top of the Himalayas to the bottom of the ocean. The triumphant soldiers and the mad civilians who shot him also grabbed Jasmine and were about to throw her in the lake next to the house when one of the leaders yelled out, "She's only a child. She has done nothing wrong. Let her be." And just like that, her life was spared, for better or for worse.

After the murder of her father, Jasmine and her younger sister spent much of their childhood with their grandparents in a rural mountain village. Their mother left for the city in search of work and eventually married into a new family. As a result, Jasmine spent the remainder of her childhood without her parents. Living as a young child without parents in a war-torn country was unimaginably difficult. One day, news arrived that her mother had successfully convinced her new husband to allow Jasmine to come live with them. At first, Jasmine refused her own mother's invitation because it didn't extend to her younger sister, but she later conceded, thinking that it was the only way for her to make something of herself. She vowed to rescue her younger sister in the future, and she did.

Life with her new stepfamily was hard, and she functioned almost like a house servant, cooking and cleaning all day, every day, in a family that had six other children (two from her stepfather's previous marriage and four from the current marriage). Nevertheless, she persevered. She even managed to earn a little respect from her new stepfather. Sensing she needed to learn some practical skills to survive in the future, she convinced him to let her go to sewing school. It would later prove to be a wise decision, when her own family became too poor to afford adequate clothing in the winter.

Eventually, Jasmine blossomed into a beautiful young woman. By nineteen, she attracted many rich suitors, but she decided to settle down with Jang. Jasmine's thought was that starting out on an equal basis with someone would be better than using her good looks to get ahead. Jang was charming and shared a similar background with her. Both of his parents had also passed away during the war. He didn't have much, but he promised her the world. She decided, despite her mother's objections, to take a chance on him and his promises. So with her new husband's two pre-teen brothers in tow, Jasmine started a new life, and bore three children: Charlie, Steve, and Kimberly.

Jang broke his promises to Jasmine almost immediately. Male-dominance prevailed in Korean culture, and became even more evident after the war. Most men constantly mistreated their women and frequently left them. Instead of rebuilding the country by setting aside their gender differences and working together as a unit, men were too busy separating and ignoring the potential contribution of their female counterparts. Jang was no different. With two of her husband's younger brothers and three children of her own, Jasmine had to pick up odd jobs here and there to make ends meet. Food was scarce and what little she could gather went to her husband and then to his younger brothers, and then to her children, and then to herself, if she hadn't opted to save it for the next day. She knitted clothing from material acquired from her mother's occasional handouts. Sometimes she had to use her own clothing to make the necessary sweaters and pants for the family for the cold winter days. She washed army uniforms on icy winter rivers and shoveled all day on landscaping projects, only to bring home just enough money to support her family's day-to-day survival, an amount far less than what men were getting for the same amount of work. Starvation was imminent for her family if she didn't act. Sometimes she collapsed from the lack of nourishment and was carried home by locals, only to receive beatings from Jang for embarrassing him. Jang was truly sick.

Although Jang didn't have a steady job, he wouldn't come home for days. When he did, he would take whatever money

Jasmine earned and leave again the next day. Jasmine plowed on, however. Soon, with the little savings she managed to put away, she opened up a small eatery in front of a busy factory. Though she was the only one working in the eatery, she operated the new business with a ferocity and determination only a mother faced with the starvation of her children could possess. Though she hardly slept nights and her husband occasionally went on a spending binge with her money, she was able to finally make the uncertainty of day-to-day survival disappear.

Then, one day, a letter from America arrived. It was from Aunt Martha, Jang's younger sister, separated from the war. Aunt Martha had married an American GI and wanted Jang and Jasmine to come live with her. As tempting as the invitation was, Jasmine wasn't receptive to the idea at first, especially since her situation was finally improving. What if Aunt Martha wasn't reliable? What if she abandoned them? So many people Jasmine relied on had broken promises to her in the past. Could she survive in a foreign land?

Eventually, however, she decided to go, for the sake of her children's future.

At the time, going to America was next to impossible unless one had a financially stable American relative who invited them there. There were tens of thousands of requests for visas to America. After struggling for two years to straighten out the applications and spending most of Jasmine's savings on the common practice of bribing officials for the issuance of visas, the Lee family arrived in America and settled into the third floor of Aunt Martha's house in Ida Lane, Rhode Island. Jasmine had high hopes of capturing a piece of the American Dream. It was November 20, 1977.

As it turned out, Aunt Martha was a very jealous person. When she learned that Jasmine was a strong, independent woman, Aunt Martha made it her personal mission to suppress her – for what reason, no one knew. Aunt Martha succeeded in slowly manipulating Jang and his now fully-grown brothers into harassing Jasmine. The sickness was spreading. When Jang's younger brothers, the ones that Jasmine had so painstakingly raised, vowed to condemn her in front of the whole family – all to impress Aunt Martha, with her stylish Americanisms – Jasmine was left with a permanent emotional scar. Her worst fears about America had come true.

She had no place to go, no one to communicate with, and no one to turn to. Her only option was to move away, and, after countless fights with Jang, and falsely reporting to her new landlord that she only had one child, she settled her family in Ashton, Massachusetts. Landlords in the area didn't want to rent their houses to families with multiple children. Steve and Kimberly sometimes had to hide in a closet when the landlord was nearby. Thus, with only two hundred dollars in her pocket, three young children, no means of communication, no transportation, and an irresponsible and violent husband, Jasmine started a new life once again.

Through the help of Koreans she managed to locate here and there, Jasmine found some manual jobs. And she worked hard. Despite the odds, she had the chance to earn a decent living and started dreaming of security for her family. It was all she ever wanted. Her dream would be interrupted when Jang decided to go back to living near Aunt Martha. But when it again didn't work out, they eventually settled back in Massachusetts.

These moves weren't done without monumental fights between Jasmine and Jang. Fights – not quarrels or spats or arguments – but fights! By now, Jasmine was tired and drained from dealing with the sickness of her husband's family. She decided never to rely on anyone else to lead her family again, even if it killed her.

Then a lucky break came her way. She landed a job at the Britton Lighting Corporation as an entry-level lighting fixtures assembler, putting together the kind of lamps that mounted on typical office buildings. She would receive pay on a per piece basis, meaning the more she assembled, the more she would earn! It was the golden chance she was looking for. A chance to get out as much as she put in. A fair chance! An equal chance! Jasmine became the company's best assembler almost overnight. The board of directors had a special session just to watch her work. The company magazine wrote articles about her. The managers rewrote the manual after studying her moves. Jasmine channeled all the years of frustration, all the years of struggle, all the years of pain and suffering into assembling thousands of lighting fixtures in record-breaking time. She assembled so hard and so ferociously that sometimes she wouldn't eat, or even to wipe her face. Although Jang was doing the same work and bringing home less than half as big paycheck, she was happy. Despite the jealousy of her co-workers, the tireless harassment of Aunt Martha and her newly appointed pawns, the constant power struggle of her abusive husband, and her aching body, Jasmine dared to hope once again.

But, her biggest challenge had yet to come.

"Your life is in danger. You will not make it to the age of forty in the far land. You are going to America, yes? But if you can endure your 39th year and survive, your life will get better, and, in the end, you will receive all the comforts and love that you have always struggled to have. You shall be rewarded for your efforts, my child. But be aware, your fate divides in two at 39. Which way it leads no one knows."

These were the words of a frail old fortuneteller who, in traditional Korean custom, had stopped Jasmine on a busy Korean street. Jasmine had never met her before. She was startled by the old lady's intrusion, but was respectful enough to listen to the fortuneteller's predictions. Tears welled up in this strange old lady's eyes. Grateful for the fortuneteller's efforts, Jasmine offered to pay for the service, but the frail old lady refused, tightly squeezing Jasmine's hands with both of hers, and went on her way. Jasmine was thirty-five years old at the time.

The winter before she turned forty, Jasmine had yet another fight with Jang. The fight went on for twelve hours. It happened because she purchased a set of new couches. She wanted to replace the set of old, run-down couches that Jang had bought at a second-hand store during their first move to Massachusetts. Naturally, Jang didn't approve of the new purchase, especially since his philosophy in life was to earn little and spend less. She bought it anyway, and he was livid. He became so angry that he wanted to dominate her, once and for all, to show her who was the boss in the family, to show her what God had intended a man's and woman's place to be.

But this time Jasmine was ready.

The fight started in the early evening and lasted through the next morning. Sometimes they wrestled and hit each other. This time, however Jasmine actually hit back, which made Jang even more ferocious. Kimberly and Steve went between them to stop them. At one point Jasmine and Jang held knives, threatening to kill each other or themselves. Only when Kimberly placed her small body between the tips of their knives did they put them down.

The fight was about more than the couches. For Jang, it was about his wife making more money than he made and his kids listening to her over him. The more his wife succeeded, the more he was reminded of his failures. He was slowly becoming invisible to his family, and he knew it. So he blamed her for it. The fight was his last desperate attempt to show her how much worse he could get, should she try to change him further. Deep down inside, however, he knew that as much as he tried to deny it, he was wrong. And though he cared about and loved her very much, for the man who spent much of his life in poverty after the war, the fine line between love and war became too intertwined for him to know the difference.

For Jasmine, the fight wasn't only about Jang's broken promises, but it was also her way of denying the deep belief that she was somehow responsible for all the misfortunes that had befallen her: the rejection from Aunt Martha, the betrayal from Jang's brothers, the broken promises of Jang, the death of her father. She wanted to let the Gods know, and let herself know, that her misfortunes weren't her fault. She was tired of feeling guilty all the time.

Eventually, Jasmine was getting weak from dehydration, but she didn't lack in energy. At times, she hyperventilated and her eyes rolled to the back of her head. Though she could hardly stand on her own, her shouting continued to resonate throughout the house. She was heading toward the big crash. Finally, in the middle of the fight, she bolted out of the house, staggering. No one knew what to do. She never physically ran from a fight before. As she stormed out, her eyes looked as if all the light had gone out from them.

Steve grabbed Jasmine's coat and was ready to go after Jasmine, but stopped in his tracks at the sight of Jang sitting on the new living room couch, the one that caused the fight to start. Something stirred in Steve.

"Dad, all Mother ever wanted were simple things. Simple things! Why can't you understand that? Why couldn't you make her happy? Why is it so hard?"

Startled, Jang raised his head and stared at Steve and was ready to shout back but eventually, to Steve's surprise, lowered his head again, this time even further.

"I don't know...I just don't know anymore," he said and spoke no more.

That was the moment when Steve, then a sophomore in high school, stopped being an obedient son to Jang.

Steve then ran outside to find Jasmine. He was worried she might catch pneumonia in her exhausted and dehydrated state. It was a very cold winter day. Or, even worse, she might collapse somewhere and freeze to death. He had to find her fast.

Holding her coat, Steve ran everywhere looking for Jasmine. While running across a tall bridge, a sudden thought hit him like a brick on the back of his head. A cold chill rushed through his body, penetrating his skin as if he were naked. He stood there frozen, in sheer terror, for what seemed like an eternity. Finally, he decided to look down the river. With his breaths heaving uncontrollably, he closed his eyes and leaned over the edge of the railing. He promised to be strong, to face the situation like a person should, to not run away in the face of challenge like Jang did, and opened his eyes. Shivers ran through him, but in the quick glance before he shut his eyes again, he saw nothing! A few more glances like that, and still nothing! He wanted to run back home but summoned his courage and checked a few more spots, and, of course, the other side of the bridge. It was the most frightening experience of his life.

Jang changed dramatically from that point on. He even cried to Jasmine asking for her forgiveness. For the first time in his life he was on his knees, begging for redemption. This macho man, a man who could do no wrong, finally admitted how invisible he had been. And, over the course of time, his complaints about working, his complaints about having tedious responsibilities, his complaints about taking care of his family, his complaints about his failure to carry out what God intended for great men like him to do, and his complaints about his wife for all his fallen dreams, slowly subsided. The Lee family was on their way to prosperity. Though his sickness never completely left him, Jasmine successfully contained it. She had won, despite how foolish she might've been to bark at the moon.

CHAPTER SIX
to catherlina

The trip to the beach, which was just a couple exits off I-782 North, took about forty minutes and consisted mostly of easy highway driving. The Lee family had used this road on their way to picnics years ago, usually with other Korean families. One of Steve's favorite part of the trip was when they stopped at convenience stores to load up on goods. He would request anything in the store and his parents would get it in a heartbeat. The picnics at the sea were always memorable for him. The smell of the sea never failed to flutter his heart while the tasty food never failed to satiate his stomach. It usually would take more than a couple of hours before everyone could find parking spaces, choose a suitable picnic area, start up a grill, prepare and grill the Bulgogi (a traditional Korean barbecue meat) at just the right temperature, unpack and set up the table with Kimbop (Korean-style sushi rolls), side dishes, beer, soda pop, Bohricha (a barley tea that can be taken hot or cold), and finally, corral all the people who by then had spread to every part of the beach. After eating, Steve usually spent his time looking at the ocean. He liked how the colors of water and sky changed at different times of the day. He often imagined he could capture the scene if only he had a camera, snapping imaginary photographs framed by his thumbs and forefingers with the click of his tongue.

Steve decided to tell Jang about Charlie. For the sake of their mission, he needed to know.

"Dad, the reason why I decided to bring Brother home is because... uh... well... because he might be doing drugs."

Steve felt like he was in a movie. This type of scene was something he had watched on TV many times before.

"I am not sure how bad he is, but I think it could be serious. So try not to scold him. We should just try to bring him home."

"Whatever. You guys can do whatever you want," Jang said tersely.

Steve wasn't sure if Jang had gotten the message. He seemed to take the news too easily. Steve had to make sure. He knew that saying it twice would sufficiently express his strong concern as he usually didn't bother to repeat things to Jang.

"Really. Don't scold him. We are talking about drugs here. Benny wouldn't have come to us if it wasn't serious. Control yourself and let's bring him home."

Jang pushed the lighter button and pulled out a cigarette from his shirt pocket. As soon as the lighter popped out, as if on cue, he let out a deep sigh and reached for it. He lit the cigarette, took a puff and then a long drag, expanding his chest to take in an extra gulp of air. He let out the smoke slowly, his face scrunching up like a brown paper bag. It was the perfect act of the Marlboro Man in agony, the macho man in distress. For a brief moment, Steve wondered what the world would be like without cigarettes. How could these men display their affliction so poetically? What a real agony that would be.

Feeling mildly satisfied with Jang's silence, Steve checked into the small lunch bag Jasmine had packed for him. Two bunches of seedless green grapes were wrapped nicely in paper towels. Perfect, he thought, grapes were exactly the food needed in his current, stressed-out condition. Steve offered the grapes to Jang, who refused, but not before letting out another sigh. Steve took out one of the two bunches for himself. The other was for Charlie. Charlie loved grapes, especially seedless green grapes. "God's gift to lazy shits like me," Charlie had once said. Somehow, though, Steve couldn't – or maybe didn't dare to – envision Charlie happily eating his fresh grapes, riding back home with him, smiling and asking, "what's for dinner?"

The last time Steve saw Charlie they had a fistfight. Steve was on his winter break from college, working for Charlie as a last minute substitute cashier in the self-service gas station Charlie managed. Charlie was supposed to relieve Steve at midnight so that he could go to another job in the morning, but Charlie was gambling in Atlantic City and didn't show up until early the next morning. Charlie drove up to one of the gas pumps in a fancy vehicle not even acknowledging Steve's stare. Steve came out of the booth to express his frustration only to receive a punch from Charlie. Steve fought back. It was against Korean custom for a younger brother to fight his older brother, but this time he didn't care. Steve never liked to transfer his frustration into physical outbursts because it reminded him of Jang, but Charlie managed to make him do otherwise.

Now Steve was going to see Charlie again and perhaps have another fight. Could he handle it? Steve cringed. The more he thought about it, the more he realized how difficult this mission might be. He was about to start a fight no one could win. Even more infuriating was the fact that he had to go and see Charlie as if he cared about him. These days Steve couldn't even stand the thought of Charlie, let alone actually care about him. He struggled with the idea of even appearing like he cared. In fact, Steve didn't want anything to do with Charlie ever again. He certainly didn't ask to be Charlie's guardian. The older brother should take care of the younger brother, not the other way around.

They took an exit off I-782 and drove on to Route 61, which stretched about 15 miles due east, leading directly to Catherlina Beach. Luckily the traffic was light, though the dirt road stirred up plenty of dust in the air. More vehicles were leaving the beach than were heading towards it, coughing up tons of black smoke that didn't dissolve well in the humid air. The dusty road, the black smoke, the old buildings, and the sweltering heat of the summer foreshadowed the trouble Steve was about to encounter.

"Since when did the trip to the beach become so ugly?" Steve wondered.

CHAPTER SEVEN
the corvette

The sun had faded well into the west by the time they reached the entrance of Catherlina Beach. Festive colors were all around the famed recreational spot. On the right side of the road was the giant Ferris wheel, decorated in red, white, and blue, going around and around to Looney Tunes music, setting the tempo for the amusement park surrounding it. On the left side were fake trees, ornaments, and the comical buildings decorating a twenty-five-hole miniature golf course. People were everywhere: some in line for food, some waiting for rides, some eating, some playing frisbee, some running, and some shopping at street vendors. All of them seemed to be working too hard to be having fun.

Route 61, which turned into Catherlina Beach Road near the shoreline, came to an end with four wood-carved signs with cartoon hands pointing to different destinations: the picnic area, the Carnival, the beach, and the shopping centers downtown. Before Steve could decide where to begin the search, Jang took a left turn towards the shopping centers, and then another detour off the main road. They ended up on a small nameless dirt road. Surrounded by wilderness, the road seemed deserted.

After a few more miles, they came to a few rows of sparsely placed houses, all needing paint jobs and new screens. Sand flew everywhere – on the street, the doorsteps, the alleyways, even on the laundry lines adorned with clean, drying clothes that seemed to stretch for miles. Jang parked his vehicle on the curb of a big, yellow, Victorian house with lots of porches and wrap-around stairs. Most of the houses in the area, though much smaller than this one, had elaborate porches and stairways. A few of them were occupied by men in clad undershirts, smoking. Something told Steve that they weren't there to relax. Their itty-bitty eyes glared at Jang's vehicle like a cat hunting a mouse.

Steve got out of the vehicle as coolly as he could. He could still smell the faint sea breeze. Instead of feeling nostalgic, however, he only felt cold sweat forming on his forehead like when as a child he used to suffer from motion sickness from bus rides. He had it so badly that he couldn't go anywhere, which turned Steve into a homebody. Even though he was eventually able to kick the problem, home had become Steve's safe haven for more reasons than one. Right now that was where he wanted to be, lying on his bed in a fetal position and sleeping until the troubles of the night disappeared.

"Well, this is where Charlie lives," said Jang, gazing at the yellow house.

Many of its doors had numbers, like a motel. Steve wondered how Jang knew where Charlie lived. Had he known all along? He probably did – Jang had known where Charlie was all along! Even after all these years, this man's lack of responsibility continued to surprise Steve.

They went around the side of the house and walked down the stairs to the basement units. Benny didn't come out of his vehicle. Jang led the way the entire time, moving very casually. Before Steve could realize what was going on, Jang was knocking on a door to the far left, the very corner of the house.

Bang, bang, bang, bang...bang, bang, bang, bang...bang, bang, bang..bang, bang, bang, bang, bang, bang, bang....

Jang knocked enough times to break the door down, but no one answered. Some profanities came from the back of the house. Steve kept his eyes on the curtain of the window for any movement inside. Maybe Charlie knew they were coming and decided to play hide and seek. The dark, thick, blue curtain, the kind that could block out even the brightest sun light, the kind that night owls like thieves, drug dealers, convicts, prostitutes, and gamblers needed for daytime sleep, wasn't moving, however.

Jang continued to bang on the door. *Bang, bang, bang, bang, bang, bang, bang, bang, bang, bang, bang, bang....*

Charlie wasn't home.

"Well, he isn't here," said Jang, talking to himself. "Gee, why isn't he here? Am I at the right house?"

Steve thought, "Am I at the right house? Am I at the right house? You mean you aren't sure? After knocking a hundred times! What if there was a very nervous drug dealer on the other side of the door, his itchy finger fondling the trigger of a sawed-off shotgun, speculating that this was a drug bust? Who else would bang on the door a hundred times?!"

To Steve, this old, run-down house looked a lot like the ones he had seen on TV, where gangs fought, with piercing bullets, for territorial rights. This apartment complex wasn't rented by civilized, law-abiding citizens looking for a weekend getaway. No sir! This was for street hustlers, the down-and-outs looking to cash in on the vacationers, legally or illegally. As much as Steve tried to keep his fear in check, he was shrinking into a tiny speck of dust with each passing second.

"Maybe we should knock on other doors, as well," said Jang.

Steve didn't say anything; he couldn't. As simple as it sounded, knocking on strangers' doors in this particular place seemed suicidal.

Nevertheless, Steve knew that was what they needed to do. He was hoping Jang would carry out the task by himself, but the rest of the apartments were located closer to him, on the right. It was Steve's turn to knock. He slowly walked over to the next door. After thinking what he would say if someone other than Charlie answered the door, or if Charlie himself answered it, he knocked – the first lightly, the second stronger, and the third lightly again. The curtain in this apartment was the same as the first.

No answer.

Steve was relieved briefly before anxiety took over again. After waiting for what he believed to be a sufficient time, he knocked again, louder. And again. He kept it to three knocks at a time, hoping the magic number would whisk away all the troubles.

Instead, however, all he heard were more profanities coming from the back of the house.

Steve was grudgingly calculating how many more doors he still needed to knock on when Jang yelled out from the first apartment. "He ain't here. I am pretty sure this is his place. I think he might've gone to the beach."

"Are you sure?"

"I think so. Yeah, it can't be any other. I am pretty sure now."

"How did you know about this place?"

"Oh, he brought me here once after fishing."

"When was that?"

"Last month."

"Last month?"

"Yeah, or sometime around then."

"You saw Charlie last month?"

"I told you 'yeah.' Why?"

Steve couldn't believe Jang's ignorance. Why didn't Jang talk to Charlie about coming home at that time?

Despite his frustration, Steve also felt some relief. Charlie couldn't be in that bad of a shape if he still spent his time fishing with Jang. Fishing calms people. You had to be sane to want to calm yourself, right?

Steve thought of his options. Should he wait for Charlie here or go look for him at the beach? It would be impossible to find him amidst the hundreds of people on the shoreline, or at the park, or at the shopping malls. His best bet might be to wait for him here. But what if he didn't show up? Also, Charlie could've moved to a different apartment. Steve didn't want to wait. He had waited long enough. He didn't come here to wait. He came to seek.

"I'll be right back, Dad. You can wait in the car," Steve said as he hopped off the stairs and walked towards the back of the house where the complaints about their knocking had come. Every cell in his body begged him to get out of this place as quickly as possible, but he had to make sure.

As Steve went up the stairs to the second floor porch, he was met by two large men with Harley Davidson muscle shirts, their guts bulging out underneath. They wore thick boots even in the heat. With their glazed eyes and long goatees, the Harley gang looked very intimidating. Again, Steve felt as though he were in a movie.

"Hi, I am looking for a guy named Charlie who lives here. Do you know him?" Steve asked.

"What?" said the larger of the two. His voice grumbled deep in his throat.

"I'm looking for a guy named Charlie. I was just wondering if you knew him."

"Nope, dunno any guy by that name here."

"Oh, you mean that skinny Chinese guy who owned the Corvette over there? I don't know him. Do you know him?" the smaller one said, turning his head towards his friend. They both had smirks on their faces – the smile of conspiratorial superiority.

Chinese guy. The smaller one reminded Steve of so many ignorant Americans who thought every person with slanted eyes was Chinese. Steve spent a good part of his existence in America explaining to people that Asia was made up of many countries, not just China, and that not all Asians talked with funny accents, practiced Kung Fu, and ate rice all day. Some never listened. To them, America was the center of the universe.

"Were you the one banging on the fucking house?" asked the larger one, flexing his biceps and giving him a peek at his elaborate tattoos.

"I was only knocking on my brother's door."

"Shit, you must've been banging on that door for an hour. Can't you take a hint that maybe the guy ain't home?"

The larger one was beginning to sound hostile. Steve needed to diffuse the situation. The next words came out of Steve's mouth faster than he could think.

"This is a family emergency." Then he added, "My father,

my friend, and I have been looking for him for a while."

Steve fought hard to maintain his composure. He looked straight into the larger one's eyes. He stared back at Steve before turning to look at the smaller one, who failed to return his friend's gaze.

"Oh, well, I didn't see him today," said the smaller one.

Steve wondered how drunk they were. Crushed beer cans were scattered all around the porch. Although the smell of the alcohol shot up his nostrils, the body odor of the two gorillas was far worse. The larger one took a long swig, crushed the can in his hands, and, looking up, yelled to someone on the upstairs porch. He momentarily lost his balance and stumbled a few steps, kicking some of the cans.

"Hey, Jake. You seen that *Chinese guy* who owns that Corvette over there lately?"

Steve got the definite impression that to these bathless wonders, the existence of the Corvette was far more remarkable than any Chinese guy.

No reply came from above.

Steve looked up. He didn't see anybody up there. He looked back at the two men. Their goatees were crooked from the smirks that had never left their faces. Steve suddenly wondered if these guys were stalling for time before deciding what to do with him. His instincts told him to retreat. They had the territorial advantage. He needed more space to handle them, to use his quickness against their size. If they attacked him here, he would be nothing more than a sitting duck. All they had to do was grab him and pin him down. He couldn't defend himself against that. Maybe one, but not two. Christ, they could crush him from solely using the weight of their beached whale bodies.

"Well, thanks anyway," Steve said and walked down the stairs.

One of them mumbled something like "wait a minute," but Steve kept going without looking back. Though he was prepared for any confrontation, his objective was to find Charlie and bring him home. But if he ever found out that these two had something to do with Charlie, then he would come back for them.

Steve could hear the faint sound of the men cackling as he stepped around the side of the house which made him wonder what was so funny about someone looking for his brother? Or did they feel sufficiently macho from scaring him off? He could only shake his head and search for a parking lot, hoping to find Charlie's Corvette even though he thought it had been repossessed long ago. The only parking lot he could see was about fifty yards from where Jang had parked. As Steve headed in that direction, so did Jang. Jang's pace soon quickened, as though he had spotted something. Benny followed.

Charlie's Corvette was in fact parked there. Jang tried to open the doors, fiddled with the trunk, and kicked the tires. Meanwhile, Steve was busy wondering how Charlie got his vehicle back, but, even more so, his whereabouts. Maybe Charlie had spotted them and had gone into hiding. Steve walked around the area, well aware of people watching them. These fugitives didn't seem too happy with the strangers in their hideouts.

"He's not here," yelled Jang, who was also searching the area. "He must be near here if his car is here, but we can't look for him all day." Perhaps he, too, had become aware of the agitated hoodlums staring at him.

Steve went back to the parking lot, hoping to find something in the vehicle that would give him clues to where Charlie might be. Parked alongside many old vehicles, the Corvette didn't stand out as much as it should've. It had enough dust to write words on it. The inside was full of stuff: clothing, boxes, papers, paper cups, napkins, food wrappers, fishing equipment, a radio, and more clothing. There was barely enough room for a driver.

Steve remembered when Charlie brought it to the house last year for the first time. He forced everyone to come out and see it, interrupting the family dinner. They were all surprised. The shiny, white convertible did look appealing on the driveway, reflecting the sunset that cast a fiery glow around the gleaming contours of its 340 horse-powered engine.

Jasmine and Steve did their best to look excited for Charlie while silently wondering where Charlie had gotten the money to buy such an expensive vehicle. They knew Charlie didn't have that kind of credit. In fact, Steve was sick to his stomach. Charlie had bought the vehicle at a time when the family needed every dollar. No doubt to impress people, people who couldn't care less about the Lee family. The vehicle symbolized everything Steve hated about Charlie.

Only Jang was genuinely impressed. To him, here was his son, all grown up and successful, bringing home one of life's highest marks of success at such a young age! Jang didn't care how Charlie got it, only that he had gotten it. Although there were countless arguments between them on issues too trivial for anyone to remember, in this instance, when he had a chance to lay down the law as a father, to talk to his son about the consequences of actions, he blew it by giving Charlie a friendly slap on the back and asking him for a joyride. Charlie officially sealed the family's approval by introducing Jang to the high wind at 90 miles per hour in the front seat of a brand new convertible Corvette. As the sound of the rough engine faded down the street, all Jasmine and Steve could do was look at each other.

"Get in the car," said Jang. It seemed he had another idea where Charlie might be. In fact, he sounded so confident this time, Steve became optimistic. They backtracked down the small road and turned towards the south part of the beach.

CHAPTER EIGHT
wooden faces

The southern part of Catherlina Beach, located about five miles away from the main recreational area, received considerably less attention from tourists because of its pointy rocks, rough sand, swamps, and wild forest. It also collected endless loads of thick sea debris and insects of every kind. The beach itself wasn't large. It certainly lacked the miles of smooth sand and open sea one would expect from a beach.

The main attraction of the area was the extended bay at the far west end that stretched for about half a mile. The bay was composed of giant rocks and cut deep into the sea, making it possible for fishermen to go fishing without a boat. Many local fishermen and their families passed their time there, as did the Lee family. Although it was mostly locals who frequented the place, on a busy day the area could still be packed.

It was here that Steve had his first fishing experience nine years ago. He did it because he wanted to know why Jang and Charlie liked it so much. They were so into it that they religiously watched hours of the Bass Master series every Saturday afternoon on TV. Typical excitement on the show consisted of a replay of a large man reeling in a big fish in super slo-mo accompanied by rocking music. For the life of him, Steve couldn't figure out what made that so exciting. Something was fishy.

Steve didn't even have a fishing pole with him at the time. It was a momentary decision, made after watching all the people on the bay repeatedly going through what he thought was a mindless process – throwing their lines in the ocean, reeling them in, throwing them in again, reeling them in, until some dumb fish bit. But these people expressed so much joy, so much contentment from a good catch, as if they were hypnotized by the magic of the ocean, that Steve suddenly wanted to experience what it was all about before deriving any further criticism about the whole thing. He wanted to see if he could be one with the ocean, too.

So Steve found a small tree branch, strong enough for a good sturdy reeling, and proudly announced to the world that he wanted to fish. Jang and Charlie were kind enough to set Steve's rod up and showed him how to hook a sea worm. Steve witnessed how Charlie hooked the worm: first through its mouth, then through the entire length of its body, until the pointy hook came out of its tail, turning the worm into the shape of the hook, its body as rigid as the steel itself. The poor sea worm wriggled helplessly, as it tried desperately to stop Charlie by curling its small body around his fingers. Steve was horrified. Imagine...a pointy hook going through its mouth and coming out the other end...still alive...tossed into the sea...to be chewed by monsters with hundreds of teeth...to be forgotten forever...receiving not a tiny bit of sympathy...why? Obviously, Charlie didn't care. He didn't even flinch. Steve had to look at him twice just to make sure that he was the normal, kind person who was also his dear brother, and not some nut who killed and mutilated for fun.

Still, Steve did his best to hide his feelings. After all, this was one of those Man Things. In fact, he even forced himself to try to hook one by himself. Fancying himself an expert fisherman, he tried to hook a worm in the same matter-of-fact manner that Charlie had. He pushed away the overwhelming feeling of guilt from killing the poor sea worm in the worst way imaginable and tried to concentrate on the pleasure of his newly-acquired hobby. What if these worms had feelings? What about their families? Did the others in the box know of their imminent demise? Isn't all life special? What had he done to deserve more than these worms, other than the fact that he was born a human being? Steve glanced at Jasmine, and gave her the most loving gaze a son could give his mother.

For a moment, Steve had wanted to free all the worms in the bait box but didn't. Jang and Charlie would've been very angry. It had been difficult for them to get the bait. The store had been crowded with fishermen, and almost all the good bait was gone. One of the worms appeared from the bait box. The slimy, long, eyeless creature curled its crimson red body ominously, as if threatening to wrap its body around Steve's neck and choke him to death for what he had done to its friend. Steve jumped back involuntarily and struggled hard to refrain from stepping on the box as hard as he could.

After hooking the worm, he found a good spot, lowered his rod, sat on a rock, and relaxed. Being on the ocean felt different this time, as if the line he dropped somehow connected him to it. He didn't feel like a spectator of the ocean this time but a participant, no longer the photographer but the photograph itself. He marveled at his Tom Sawyer-like fishing rod. Everything seemed perfect. Sitting on the bay, passing time with a self-made fishing pole, picnicking with loved ones at the edge of the great Atlantic Ocean, his stomach full and mind adventurous, watching the sultry wind seduce the reflection of the dancing sun high on the horizon. Steve concluded that this was what fishing was all about. It had nothing to do with the fish. He could begin to like this, he thought.

There was movement underneath and within seconds his fishing rod shook violently, almost bending in half. Steve instinctively lifted his fishing rod, not knowing what to feel. He decided to grab the line directly lest the rod break in half. After some effort, he managed to pull the fish out of the water. It was a small bluefish, which were plentiful at that time of the year. Judging from its resistance, he expected a bigger fish. He was amazed at the strength of the fish, struggling for its dear life – the last struggle before its inevitable death. Steve wondered how much of a fight he could generate if he was in the same position. He wanted to cut the line and let the fish go, but Charlie was already running toward him to help out.

Jang and Charlie seemed more excited than Steve. Charlie immediately secured the flapping fish and unhooked its mouth.

Blood poured out of its punctured mouth and heaving gills. Its body kept flapping violently until Charlie finally dropped it in a bucket. Only then could Steve exhale, temporarily relieved that at least the fish could breathe again. The shake of his rod and the struggle of the fish felt too real to him.

Jang gave Steve one of the biggest smiles that Steve had seen from him and some complimentary words like "that's my boy," "chip off the old block," or "the boy wonder." Charlie's murmurs were more contemporary, like "awesome," "cool," "all right," "fuckin' A." Steve couldn't remember ever having been complimented so much by both of them at the same time. As bad as he felt for the fish, it felt good to be in the center of Jang and Charlie's world. It didn't happen every day.

Charlie then immediately hooked another worm onto Steve's line. Jang grabbed the bucket to show Steve's catch to the other families. All of them gave Steve a smile and thumbs-up signs. Even Jasmine smiled. Steve thought this was far better than receiving a straight-A report card! He could conclude only one thing from all this – the Bass Master has awakened!

And he kept catching more. There must've had been some kind of bluefish colony where he dropped his line because a great many of them, large and small, kept biting his stick to Hell all day long. Each and every time, Jang and Charlie would take turns helping Steve retrieve the fish and hook another worm. Their compliments were just as lauded as the first time. Jang even interrupted his beer drinking to help. Charlie ran over from the far end of the bay to help, risking a dangerous fall. And all Steve had to do was reel in when his line shook.

He also noticed their expressions as they methodically reset his line. Stern, wooden expressions that wouldn't bat an eyelash even in the face of death. Men who could kill without remorse. Men who could die without fear. Men who could survive any condition using only their bare hands. The true essence of men, undiminished by the existence of computers and suits and ties. The way Mother Nature wanted her sons to be. While Steve's heart skipped a beat each time he caught a fish, Jang and Charlie were calm, skillful, knowledgeable, and purposeful in their task, as if the end of world wouldn't faze them. They looked so...strong. Steve realized then, even at the center of Jang's and Charlie's world, he could never wear their expressions no matter how hard he tried. That was the last time Steve fished. It wasn't for him. One thing was for sure, he wasn't going to eat the fish he caught.

CHAPTER NINE
elle

Steve, Jang, and Benny arrived at the southern part of Catherlina Beach around seven-thirty. They parked on the east side of the beach in the only available parking lot. Not many vehicles were parked there as most visitors had already left.

Some old, run-down houses lined the small, winding road, the only one accessible to this part of the beach. There were a handful of people around the beachfront houses, mostly kids. The bay area, where Steve had fished with Jang and Charlie, was about three hundred yards across from the parking lot, cutting through the beach. Jang seemed confident that Charlie could be found there, and now, somehow, Steve was too.

"You think Charlie's at the bay?" Steve asked.

"I don't know. Maybe. If he's not here, I don't know where he might be," Jang replied.

Steve turned to Benny.

"What's up, Benny? Doing all right?"

"Yeah, mang. Everything's cool."

"Watch out for the pointy rocks," said Jang, as he took the first step to the sand.

Steve looked forward to walking on the beach. The sound of the waves, the familiar cry of the sea birds, and the open sea could lift his spirits a little.

The sun grew more magnificent as it slowly set. Red arrows from the waning sunlight hit all around the beach. The last time Steve was here was with his high school girlfriend Elle, during his summer break from college. Her long, white, soft, summer skirt swayed gently in the wind as she walked carelessly next to him, hand in hand. She smelled nice, too. He was full of exciting stories about his new college life. She was quiet and courteous, replying when necessary, smiling when appropriate, but sentimental about their separate lives.

Although Steve had spent only a year in college, the new life made him somewhat bold. He teased her about not wanting to have sex with him. She smiled and replied that she didn't want to have sex with him. She wanted to make love to him, and only if and when the time was right. She said making love had to be special. It was important to her. He joked again saying that he guessed he wasn't so special to her. She answered only with silence and gripped his hand a little tighter.

Steve didn't push the subject further. Not because he had never made love to a woman before and wouldn't have known how to do it very well, but because he hadn't known the difference between making love and having sex. As usual, Elle was talking about something far more mature than he was capable of understanding, but without making him feel inferior. She was always good at that. Occasionally, Elle planted her warm, moist lips on Steve's. She was sad to see him go so far away. Even sadder to see him changing. They sat on the beach exchanging few words until the sun went down and only its glow held the twilight of the dusk. Everything had an ending. Even their kisses and tender touches. Elle cried quietly, giving him a taste of her tears in their kisses. Her long hair cascaded down, splashing its silkiness onto their softly locked lips.

The fact was that Elle always felt guilty that her Italian father didn't approve of Steve, just because he was Asian. During their rare dates, Steve would have to drop her off one block from her house and watch her walk home alone, so her father wouldn't see them together. Elle was two years younger than he was and didn't have a vehicle. Many times, Steve had to ask his best friend Vincent, who was Italian, to pick her up from her house before Steve could take her out. The whole situation frustrated him, infuriated him, but he had no choice. He cared about her very much, and he would've done anything to see her then. She was his first love, his first kiss, and he, hers.

But the moment Steve entered college, things began to change. The diversity of the student body allowed him to explore his own culture. Steve saw fellow Asians daily: in the streets, stores, classrooms, cafeterias, libraries, and even in martial arts practices. They were everywhere. Also, many of them shared his background: born in Korea but raised in the United States, coping with the differences between the two cultures, and sometimes feeling alienated by both.

Steve was even able to sharpen his native language skills and enjoy Korean pop culture, especially Korean songs, old and new. The music, the lyrics, the melody succeeded in shredding the walls of assimilation Steve had built in America. They were so understanding and sympathetic to his history, reminding him of a time when he knew nothing of racism and cynicism, when life was simple. He didn't know what he had missed. For the first time, Steve could be in a group of friends without feeling different. It was as if his country had come to him because he couldn't go to his country, an experience he thought he could never have in America.

Steve felt very close to his new Asian friends, and easily identified with them. As special as Elle was to him, he was slowly gaining urges to explore the girls of his culture – the girls who could speak his native language, the girls who could understand him more, the girls who could potentially cut his soul deep like the native songs he discovered...or even deeper.

The following semester, Steve received this letter from Elle:

Dear Steve,

The leaves are falling, Steve - with each leaf passes yet another minute, another precious moment of your life, my life. The wind chases the fire from the moon. The white moon, dull, passive, cannot chase the fire. She can only let it pass. The fire is free, so the moon must also be free. Each in their

separate worlds. Remember the flowers,
Steve. Remember the moon, but do not let
them hold you back. For I am the moon,
Steve, and you are the fire. They are both
free.... - Elle
P.S. Please call me.

Steve called her. They exchanged nice words, shared their thoughts, reminisced about their wonderful times together, and, after a tearful farewell from Elle, they hung up and went their separate ways. Steve was thankful for how easy she made the whole affair. She was always a step ahead of him, had done things for him that improved him. He wondered if he could ever meet someone like her again.

As attractive as Elle was, it was her mind and her words Steve cherished the most. He kept all her letters, neatly stacked away in his treasure box. From time to time, he would come across her letters and read them, reflecting, smiling, sometimes saddened. Elle's letters were priceless and timeless. From her, Steve learned the difference between making love and having sex. Though Steve never had sex with her, he was sure they made love before. Once again, Elle had shown him something very mature, but without making him feel inferior. She was always good at that.

Sex is the love of the body, and love is the sex of the mind.

Staring now at the open sea with Jang and Benny, Steve wondered where she was and what she was doing. What would she think of him now? Would he be in her thoughts at all? He marveled at the twists and turns of life. The passage of time seemed so cruel. Here he was once again, but now for a completely different reason. Even the beach seemed to acknowledge that: the sea birds, the sound of the waves, and the waning sunlight only alarmed him of the little time he had left to find Charlie. The innocence of romance was a luxury Steve could no longer afford. Welcome to the real world, he thought, the adventures of Tom Sawyer were over.

CHAPTER TEN
the encounter

Jang noticed Charlie first. In the outstretched red sun, two silhouettes emerged. Jang waved at them. One of the two figures waved back, and the two continued their walk towards them. They were both holding fishing rods, and one also held a bucket. Slowly, the figures became clearer. Steve could now see the colors of their clothes. His stomach tightened. One of the figures was unfamiliar to him, but the other was indeed Charlie, smiling.

Charlie looked good. He wore a navy blue sweatshirt he had gotten from Disney World last winter and a pair of gray Dickies pants, which momentarily amused Steve. Steve remembered how Charlie came home one day, very excited to tell him about these new pants he discovered through his friends at his junior high school: Dickies didn't wrinkle no matter how much they were worn. Not that Charlie, at that age, cared whether his pants wrinkled or not, but the fuss of the marketing got to him. He was so excited that Steve got excited, too. Both of them gulped at the thought of owning a pair.

Charlie had a deep, dark tan. Although his hair shined from a greasy sheen, he looked healthy and relaxed. There was no question that Charlie spent much of his time at the beach. His presence fit well here. Charlie didn't acknowledge Steve, but instead turned to greet Jang. Charlie's face became wooden.

"Catch anything good?" asked Jang, in a rather melodic voice.

It was the required greeting of any true fisherman. Steve knew Jang was genuinely curious. Jang and Charlie could talk about fishing for hours, even in the midst of World War III.

"Not much. It's hard this time of the year. That guy over there got a big catch," said Charlie, pointing to a lonely fisherman reeling in his rod at the shoreline. Why was he not fishing at the bay? Steve wondered.

Jang peeked into Charlie's bucket. Steve took a peek, too, wondering if Charlie ever ate the fish he caught. The bucket was empty. The wind gained momentum and whipped through everyone's hair, further disguising the purpose of their encounter.

As usual, Charlie neglected to introduce his friend. Charlie never liked formalities because to him formalities only hid one's true intentions. Not that Steve wanted to know who Charlie's friend was – probably just another hoodlum-Charlie-worshipper looking for a handout; Charlie's toy soldier.

"I caught some small ones, but I let them go. I really came here to relax," said Charlie, seeming a little defensive after Steve and Jang peeked into his empty bucket.

"What bites nowadays?" asked Jang.

"Mackerel," said Charlie.

"Mackerel? I thought this was bluefish season," said Jang.

"No, not anymore. It's mackerel now. But it's hard to find any in the low tide. High tide should come by late tonight. Night fishing has been really good here this week," said Charlie.

"That sounds swell," said Jang.

"I went a few times last week...." The voices of Charlie and Jang slowly faded from Steve as he focused all his energy on fighting to maintain his composure. He felt out of place. Around the two fishermen talking about their passion, he felt like a wimpy boy who couldn't even hold his stomach near flapping fish, nor the sight of hooking a sea worm. There seemed to be nothing wrong with Charlie. If Elle had seen this, she would've probably laughed at him.

He was relieved, though. The drug abuse couldn't have been that bad if Charlie looked so good. Charlie didn't look like those people on TV, nor was he too skinny, like Jasmine had mentioned. Maybe the purpose of their encounter no longer needed to be revealed.

Steve snapped back to reality from Jang's voice.

"How did you get here? We saw your car in the parking lot back at the main beach."

Charlie's face turned a little more serious, and he quickly glanced at Benny. Benny turned away and put his hands in his pockets. Steve noticed that Charlie continued to ignore him.

"Benny, how did they know where my car was?" asked Charlie, his tone even and controlled but with an unmistakable air of annoyance.

"I already knew where it was. I came here to look for you with Mom last month for your insurance thing," said Steve, cutting in, lying. He didn't want Benny to take the rap. He also wanted to drop a hint as to why he was here.

"How did you get here without your car?" Jang asked again, still friendly.

"With my Accord. It's my 2nd car for doing errands. I don't usually take my Vette for casual trips," said Charlie.

Steve could now detect Charlie's strain to contain his growing annoyance. Charlie wanted to get out of the situation fast.

They reached Charlie's Accord, which was only a few spaces from where Jang had parked. Steve could see that there was even more stuff in Charlie's blue Accord than in his Corvette. Maybe Charlie thought filling the vehicle with personal items further sealed whom the vehicle belonged to, especially since he knew the name on the pink slip wasn't his. Steve was sure none of the vehicles that Charlie owned actually had Charlie's name on the pink slips.

Charlie opened the trunk and quickly started disassembling his fishing equipment with precision – a ritual he had performed hundreds of times before. Although the vehicle's interior was a mess, its trunk was neatly organized, mostly with fishing equipment and a few hunting rifles. Jang, with both hands in his pockets, peeked in. Between Charlie and Jang, they had racks full of rifles, some manual, some semi-automatic, some semi-automatic that could be assembled into fully automatics like M-16's, and some shotguns, each one packing enough powder to kill a rhino. They also owned three state-of-the-art bows and arrows for deer hunting and an assortment of hunting knives, including one Steve recognized from the movie Rambo. Forget talking about fishing during World War III, Jang and Charlie could start the war themselves.

Charlie moved efficiently and within minutes had finished disassembling his and his friend's fishing rods and had them packed into their appropriate places in the trunk. If Steve didn't do something fast, Charlie would be gone soon.

But what?

"Let's go home," said Jang. "We came to take you home with us. Have a warm meal and relax." It was the voice of one fisherman to another, with as much charisma as he could muster. It even helped Steve feel at ease.

Charlie chuckled tersely. It sounded more like he was clearing his sinuses than laughing. This single action discouraged Steve beyond his wildest beliefs and brought home the reality of the situation he now must face. The suggestion of going home was so outrageous, so comical to Charlie that all he could do was laugh. The funny thing was, Steve understood that more than his own mission.

Charlie quickly finished packing the bucket and some stuff from his pockets into the trunk and slammed it shut with a loud thud.

"I have a home," said Charlie, as he turned towards the driver's side of his Accord.

Steve wanted stronger persuasion from Jang. Time was of the essence. If something didn't happen fast, Charlie would be gone, perhaps for good. As calm as the situation appeared, it was becoming critical. Steve's heart pumped so hard his entire body vibrated. But no further persuasion came from Jang.

"Yo, mang. You should go home, mang," said Benny, nonchalantly.

Funny how people can sound so normal in such

extraordinary situations, Steve thought. Steve's mind was crying out to stop Charlie, slap him around a few times, yell at him for the problems he had caused their family, and yank his sorry ass home. Yet civility prevailed, and everyone appeared calm – like a time bomb ticking away.

The locals in the beachfront houses stared at them. Perhaps they had detected something in their body language. Steve could hear a dog barking, its sound dissipating quickly into the open field.

"Shut up, Benny. I'll fuckin' deal with you later," Charlie shouted, without looking at him.

The first outburst. The cat was about to come out of the bag. Charlie stopped at the vehicle door and fumbled in his pocket for his keys. Dickies had deep pockets, deep enough to scratch your balls with full satisfaction, Charlie had once joked. Finally, he retrieved the Accord key, unlocked his door and swiftly got in. He rolled down his window to let out the heat.

Without hesitation, Steve walked toward Charlie and grabbed the door before Charlie could shut it. It was Steve who let out the cat.

"You are going home with us," said Steve, feeling rather strange with the amount of calmness he heard from his own voice.

Charlie stopped moving and stared at him for a brief moment, bewildered, as if Steve had just appeared. Their eyes met for the first time, for the first time in a very long time.

"Get outta here," said Charlie finally, turning away. His passive reaction surprised Steve, but not for long.

"Let go of the fuckin' door!" Charlie shouted, loud enough to vibrate the interior.

Charlie's face turned red and, Steve noticed, as if on cue, the reflection of the interior lights made Charlie's greasy hair look even shinier. Charlie must not have showered in weeks. Then, he noticed Charlie's weakened body frame and how his navy shirt and Dickies pants engulfed him. It was true: Charlie was indeed as skinny as Jasmine had mentioned.

Steve didn't know what to do or what to say next, so he continued to hold on to the door. Charlie started up the vehicle. His friend got into the passenger seat. Steve panicked but still held on to the door. Charlie revved his engine. Steve held on tighter, wrapping his entire arm around the door and locking it with his other arm, which hooked underneath the window frame. He envisioned his body being violently dragged away in a high-speed car chase. Charlie shifted into drive. Steve clenched his jaw.

"I'm gonna drive away. You stay like that, you're gonna get hurt," said Charlie in a low, threatening tone.

Steve said nothing.

"I'm serious! Get the fuck out of my way! Okay, fine. I'm gone," said Charlie, about to step on the gas pedal.

Just then, Jang came closer and held on to the door as well. "Hey, your brother wants to take you home for a good meal and comfort. What's the matter with you? Stop getting angry and let's go home."

Steve let out a sigh of relief. At least Charlie wouldn't drag both of them. Would he?

"Dad, get outta there, will you?" said Charlie.

"Listen, Son, let's just go home."

"Will you get out? I wanna go home."

"For crying out loud, Son! What are you doing? We came here for you. Let's go home."

"Dad, will...."

"Why are you doing this?"

"Dad, w...."

"What's the matter with you?"

"Da...."

"Don't you know we came here for you?"

"D...."

"We came to take you home."

"Holy Shit!" shouted Charlie, re-shifting his engine back to park, breathing heavily. He kept his eyes on the front windshield, obviously thinking hard for his next move. He was edgy, feeling overwhelmed by the conviction of Jang and Steve's motives – which was what? – to tell him where he should spend the night tonight? How absurd! How arrogant!

Charlie shut off his engine, got out of the vehicle, and without a word, started to walk away. Steve followed.

"Where are you going?" Jang asked, as he also tried to follow. Benny also followed. Charlie didn't answer. Instead he increased his pace, but Steve was almost neck and neck with him.

"This is really stupid. Who do you think you are, coming here and making me do what I don't want to do? You could get in trouble for that. You think you can control me?" Charlie yelled to Steve.

"I just want you to come home, man, that's all. That's all I want," Steve replied.

"Get out of here! Go home. I don't want to see your fuckin' face," said Charlie.

Aware of the distance he could gain from the group, especially Jang, Charlie started to run. Steve followed. The sound of Jang and Benny's footsteps grew distant. They were running halfheartedly, more wishing for Charlie to stop than actually chasing him. Jang continued to ask Charlie where he was going, his voice quickly waning. Soon, it was just Charlie and Steve.

Charlie turned into the backside of the beachfront houses. All of sudden, the beach turned desolate. Tall, thick weeds and dry, cracked ground ruled here. Insects flew wildly. This area was a swampland. Steve could see the highway far in the distance, about a mile down, part of Catherlina Road. Weeds grew densely in that direction.

The sun had now gone down and only the sunset held the faint light. Charlie was camouflaging well in the fast approaching darkness. It would be harder to spot Charlie in the dark, Steve thought, so he decided to stay closer to him.

Steve's heart continued to thump wildly and his mind felt

numb. Maybe all this was stupid. Maybe he had bitten off more than he could chew. It wasn't like Charlie was still a little kid. He couldn't just manhandle Charlie and hope to physically carry him home. It seemed so irrational. What the Hell was he thinking? It had felt so right when he was telling Jasmine about it. As much as he hated that macho stuff, maybe that was exactly what made him come here. He came for his own selfish ego rather than to aid Charlie. Was it not just hours ago that he thought about how he couldn't care less what happened to Charlie so long as his family was okay? Maybe he, himself, was the ultimate egomaniac of the Lee family. Maybe he was the worst sicko of the sickness that plagued the male side of the Lee family.

Steve thought about stopping. Each step felt heavy. He wanted to let Charlie go. How much more stupidity could he muster to prolong this ridiculous situation? Maybe it wasn't too late for him to apologize and just go home.

Then, suddenly Charlie stopped running and turned around to face Steve. Steve stopped. He braced himself, quickly examining the premises. One of the first things he learned from martial arts was to familiarize himself with his surroundings before engaging in any confrontation. Steve was already aware that they were in the middle of nowhere. He could see distant lights coming from the beachfront houses and hear some dogs faintly barking, reminding him of how far he was from civilization. He was sure no one came to this part of the swampland, not even the local hormone-driven teenagers looking to get drunk and get laid. This wasn't a good place to be in a fight.

Charlie walked towards him. Steve didn't backtrack. That wasn't why he was here.

"Who the fuck do you think you are, huh? Who the fuck do you think you are?" shouted Charlie, the open field swallowing his voice, making him seem more distant than he was.

"I just want to take you...."

Bang!

Steve saw a bright light in his left eye. His glasses sprung off his face. His knees buckled, and he fell, stomach first. It was a fast punch, very fast. Steve thought that after all the years of martial art training, he could've at least seen it coming. Not only was the punch faster than he could react, but it was faster than he could think, faster than he could imagine. After all, Charlie had practiced the martial art, too.

Not knowing what he should do next, Steve quickly tried to retrieve his glasses. He found them about ten feet away in a small patch of weeds. He would've never found them if it weren't for the lights of the beachfront houses reflecting in the lens. One of the lenses was missing. After making sure Charlie wasn't going to go anywhere or do anything like beat the shit out of him, he quickly searched for the missing lens. Great, he thought, I can't afford a new pair of glasses. The lenses in his glasses had been popping out of their frames for the longest time, but he kept repairing them with crazy glue.

The thought of retaliation never crossed Steve's mind. His only hope was to not receive any more punches. But if Charlie punched again, then he would have to take it. He had to show compassion. He didn't come here to fight with Charlie so that he could feel macho; he came here to take Charlie home because he cared for Charlie's well-being. *He cared for Charlie's well-being!* Somehow things were clearing up for him now, as if the punch had rattled his cloudy thoughts.

"Shit!" Charlie murmured.

Shit? Did I hear that correctly? A sound of guilt? Compassion for his fallen brother? Maybe Charlie wasn't as drugged out as Steve thought!

Charlie started running towards the highway again.

This time Steve only stood and watched. He longed for the comfort of his sofa and a good night's rest. The day was getting longer by the second. If he went after Charlie now, then there would be no turning back. He might provoke Charlie enough to drive both of them over the edge. It could even cost their lives. He could give up here while he still had the chance, especially after Charlie had shown him a hint of compassion. Steve had sent his message. Charlie now knew that the family cared and wanted him home, even after all the mistakes he had made. Wasn't that what Steve had wanted to tell Charlie in the first place? Hadn't Steve done all he could? Besides, he was half blind now.

Steve closed his eyes, tasting the trickle of blood from the corner of his mouth. Jasmine's voice came into his head:

'I didn't tell you this, but I had a terrible nightmare the other night. I saw Charlie floating lifelessly in a river. No matter what I did, I couldn't stop him from drifting downward. I need to see him. I need to see with my own eyes that he is okay. I don't think....'

Something was happening inside Steve. Something of great force. For the first time today, he felt clear. A surge of energy circulated through his entire nervous system. His legs felt light, his heart pumped evenly, and his head was clear enough to match the night sky with thousands of sparkling stars. He could even smell the scent of the sea breeze again. He would bring Charlie home, even if it killed him.

Steve opened his eyes and ran towards Charlie. The night was just beginning.

CHAPTER ELEVEN
the sweater

It was a chilly early morning in the Fall of 1972 in Hangikdong, Korea. Steve was late for school for the first time in his life. He was six years old. Unlike Charlie, Steve was a late developer, and Jasmine had worried that she might have to send him to a special school for the learning disabled. Unfortunately, she couldn't afford it. In fact, Steve was forced to skip kindergarten before entering first grade. In the struggling country, even the public elementary schools required a hefty tuition fee. Young Steve was excited about his new school life. Going to school with all his friends and doing homework with them was grown-up stuff for which Steve had waited for a long time. But being late for school, and getting into trouble for it was a new experience for him.

Charlie, who was two-and-a-half years older, was responsible for helping young Steve to school each morning. On that day, Jasmine left early with baby Kimberly to find work. Jang was in the middle of one of his disappearing acts. With no one to wake them, Charlie and Steve slept in. They hurried to put on their clothes, packed their books and ran out the door, without even having the breakfast Jasmine had prepared for them – a porous rice, Kimchi, and soy sauce.

Young Steve noticed the usual hustle and bustle of the crowd on Main Street was missing. The street was normally crowded with people going to school, going to work, or trading goods. One could hardly walk in a straight line. It was fun for Steve as he twisted and turned between people's paths, imagining himself a superhero chasing bad guys. But now, there was no crowd. The street was desolate, with only the dry leaves scratching the surface of the road. He could sense he was in deep trouble. The humming, hollow sound of the empty street deafened Steve's ears, as if the whole world hushed because of his tardiness.

Young Steve stopped in his tracks and started crying. He didn't know what the consequence of his wrongdoing would be. He never had to deal with punishments from anyone other than Jasmine before. Would he be expelled? Beaten? Killed? The harder he stared at the empty streets, the more scared he became. He knew he should run as fast as he could to school to minimize his tardiness. Even the wind seemed to push him from behind. Only, he couldn't move his legs. They were shaky and numb from fear. He wanted to run back home and hide under his thick blanket, but Charlie told him not to.

Charlie wiped the tears from young Steve's eyes.

"It's okay, Steve," said Charlie as he continued to wipe Steve's tears away with the sleeves of the sweater Jasmine had knitted. "They won't punish you that much. You won't be the only one. I see kids going to school late all the time. See that kid over there? He's late, too."

Charlie pointed his finger at a small kid walking hand-in-hand with his parents. That didn't calm Steve. At least the kid had his parents with him.

Steve tried to walk a few steps more, but his shaky legs, the humming of the empty street, and the chilly wind, cold enough to freeze his tears, stopped him once again. He was sure the teacher was going to beat him severely.

Back in those days, it wasn't unusual for school teachers to beat their students, even the good students. Some teachers beat their students so harshly that they were given nicknames. One of the teachers was nicknamed Tiger Teacher because of his notorious brutality. Steve heard stories about how this teacher would pick up a boy by his sideburns, and slam him into a desk, head first. Sometimes, for no good reason, this teacher would randomly choose some kids in the class to be whipped on the butt with baseball bats.

All of the students in Tiger Teacher's class behaved extremely well and tried to stay on his good side. They consistently earned high marks in the city-wide aptitude tests given by the government and as a result, the school's officials tolerated his radical method, if not celebrating it. No one could stop his brutality, not even the parents. It was just how things were done in those days.

Charlie had Tiger Teacher that year.

Charlie could've run to school and gotten there on time. He was one of the school's star athletes. Instead, he stayed with Steve, giving him hugs and patiently encouraging him to keep walking. Charlie kept pointing out different people on the street who were also going to be late. He even cried when Steve cried. Each and every time Steve stopped in his tracks, Charlie was there, wiping his tears, giving him hugs, and crying with him, until Steve felt well enough to continue on.

After countless stops, they finally reached the school. Charlie guided Steve to his homeroom, gave him one final hug and lightly pushed him inside. Steve walked in crying, feeling alone for the first time. All eyes were on him. Steve looked back at Charlie, wanting him to come with him. Standing in front of his class, he never felt so exposed. The teacher, who was in the middle of writing verses on the blackboard, paused, stared at him, and then told him to sit down in his chair...and that was it! There was no punishment, not even any words of warning.

Charlie stuck his head into the room, saw Steve, smiled, waved, and left. He had waited outside until he was certain that Steve wouldn't receive any cruel punishments. Steve couldn't even wave back from all the trauma. The teacher resumed writing on the board, and Steve was finally relaxed enough to open his book. It was then that Steve realized that Charlie was late as well, very late. His homeroom was at the far end of the building, four flights up. With Tiger Teacher, Charlie was doomed to be thrown into desks head first. Not once did he mention that.

Steve cried again, this time for Charlie. The pages of his textbook turned transparent from his teardrops.

The smell of Charlie's sleeve, the one that had wiped Steve's face that day so many times, came to symbolize the comfort, security, love, and nostalgia in Steve's sense of identity from that day forward. Charlie was Steve's first guardian angel.

CHAPTER TWELVE
the chase

Soon, Charlie was in Steve's sight again. Charlie had run too quickly in the beginning, and had to slow down considerably. He couldn't be in good shape, Steve thought, especially if he was doing drugs, smoking a pack a day, and fishing all the time. Steve took his time before closing the gap, pacing himself, aware of the importance of maintaining a rhythm in long-distance running. He breathed evenly, pumped his arms precisely, relaxed his body – the knowledge gained from high school track days fully appreciated. In no time, he was running right behind Charlie.

The sound of their footsteps filled the abandoned swampland, no man's land, crushing the patches of dry weeds and cracking the flaky surface formed by the hot sun. Charlie's pocket change jingled chaotically as each step of his hard-soled boat shoes clapped the ground like tap shoes. They were running like two hungry predators chasing their prey in an open prairie – so wild and free, yet so desperate.

"You can't follow me forever, Dickhead," said Charlie as he huffed and puffed.

Steve opted not to reply lest he further provoke Charlie. Charlie would soon enough appreciate Steve's determination to bring him home. Besides, the last time he tried to talk back, he got punched.

"I'm gonna be running into some crazy places. I know where the swamps are. Try to follow me if you can. I'll bury you there, Motherfucker!" said Charlie.

Motherfucker! – The word sent by the God of Low Lives as the supreme curse to be used as freely and as frequently as possible by his chosen English-speaking subjects in America. Charlie had never lowered himself to using this word on Steve until this very moment. Maybe that was because they had the same mother.

Charlie picked up his pace again. They were back on the narrow road still running away from the beach, towards the highway. No one was around. It was dark now and mosquitoes from the swampland were out in full force. The shops and restaurants had closed for the day. There was no nightlife on this part of the shoreline, not for humans, anyway. The farther they ran from the beach, the thinner the signs of civilization became.

Soon the sidewalk disappeared, and they were running on the shoulders of the barren road.

"All I have to do is go somewhere you can't go. I know you aren't legally twenty-one," panted Charlie, his words coming in short bursts.

Whoa! – What's he up to now? Steve wondered.

"I'm serious. There's a bar around the corner over there. You don't fuckin' believe me? They don't let under twenty-one assholes like you in. I'm heading over there right now. See if I'm kiddin' or not."

"Go ahead," Steve replied, confused momentarily about why he decided to answer Charlie this time. Once again, he was surprised by the amount of calmness he heard from his own voice.

Steve had gotten younger by fifteen months when he first arrived in America. The Lee family found that out when they were applying for their visas. The record department at City Hall had neglected to file Steve's birth certificate properly and as a result, Steve's age was recorded fifteen months younger than his actual age. Instead of correcting it, however, Jang decided to make Steve's new age official to take advantage of the airfare discount for children under ten. They ended up saving about a thousand dollars. Time really was money, young Steve had learned.

Steve was surprised that, not only did Charlie know this fact, but he could conjure up such a dubious plan from it, especially at a time like this. Charlie was a master plotter even in the heat of fire, maybe even especially in the heat of fire. But this time, his calculations were wrong.

"I'm serious, mang. There is a bar over there. They don't fuck around. They'll kick your motherfuckin' ass outta there if you're not over 21. They'll beat the shit out of you," Charlie yelled, renewing his strength.

"Go ahead."

"I'm going there right now. You won't make it through the door. What, you think I'm kiddin'? All I have to do is get in and make a getaway through the back. You'll never know. Better quit chasing me now, Asshole. It's useless."

"I am twenty-one."

"What? Get outta here. Don't fuckin' lie to me."

"Well, I am."

Charlie turned to look at Steve. Steve kept his eyes forward, letting Charlie stare him down. Unlike Charlie, Steve had nothing to hide, no skeletons in the closet.

"You're bullshitting me. I'm serious, mang, I'm going into the bar," said Charlie, testing Steve and hoping he was bluffing while he frantically tried to do math in his head.

"I turned twenty-one last November. You want to see my license?"

Steve longed to add: "That's right Charlie, time flies. You and I are older than we think. So stop this childish nonsense and let's go home."

Charlie stopped. So did Steve. Charlie's hands curled up into fists again and Steve braced himself for another punch. His left side still felt hot from Charlie's right hook. He avoided eye contact, knowing he had to appear subservient to Charlie at this moment. If Charlie threw any more punches, he was ready to take them. Anything…anything to increase Charlie's compassion towards him. At the same time Steve couldn't help but wince at the thought of how fast Charlie's punch was. It was fast, faster than he could see. It would be hard to brace for something like that.

"Holy Shit, what da fuck do you want from me!" shouted

Charlie, realizing Steve wasn't the type who bluffed.

With a few more motherfuckin' this and motherfuckin' that, Charlie headed towards the highway again, this time making a mad dash.

Steve followed, but again not as fast. If Charlie really wanted to scare him, Steve thought, he should've at least paced himself during his running. As usual, Charlie acted on his impulses, never thinking long-term. In no time, Steve was right behind him again as they finally reached the freeway.

While crossing an overpass bridge, panic shot through Steve's entire body. He peeked behind him for signs of any oncoming vehicles, making sure that Charlie wasn't looking at him as he did so. The highway seemed deserted, except for the sound of their footsteps on the asphalt and Charlie's heavy breaths. The sparse fluorescent streetlamps managed to discolor the remains of civilization into shades of gray. There were no vehicles on the road.

Charlie's breathing was getting out of control. His strides became erratic, causing him to lose his balance. Steve dropped back a few steps to give him room to sway. Maybe if Charlie passed out, he could just carry him home, he thought.

"I can't believe the shit you are doing to me. This is so fuckin' ridiculous. You can get into trouble for this, Asshole. Big trouble. What did I ever do to you?" panted Charlie.

What did I ever do to you? What did I ever do you? Where should I begin?

"All I want is for you to come home," said Steve, as he worried about Charlie's rapidly deteriorating condition.

"I ain't....going home, and you can't...make me. You can...get in trouble for this. Just...a...leave me alone! Who da fuck do you...think you are?" screamed Charlie, his eyes flickering like a candle in the wind as he looked at Steve again.

Steve noticed Charlie wasn't sweating much now; he was dehydrating himself.

Charlie slowed down considerably as they entered the

second overpass bridge, which was rigged with more streetlamps. Just then a large truck whizzed by on the other side of the road, generating enough wind to disrupt their strides. Steve's heart turned to ice. Somehow, he knew what Charlie was going to say next.

"If you...don't...leave me...alone, ...I'm...gonna jump...on to the next car...that comes," squealed Charlie, staggering, ready to collapse.

This time Charlie didn't use profanity. As Charlie's trembling words echoed across the caged walls of the overpass bridge, Steve's vision blurred.

Steve was aware that Charlie had suicidal tendencies. Charlie had indeed attempted to kill himself a couple of times. Once, he locked himself in a vehicle with the carbon monoxide flowing to the interior, took some tranquilizer pills to help him fall asleep faster, and parked his vehicle off some bush in a highway. Miraculously, his girlfriend, who was an EMT specialist, found him and resuscitated him. Steve and his family shuddered at the thought of the incident. To make matters worse, Steve's family dealt with each of Charlie's flirtations with death by ignoring them. It was their collective sense of denial. Now Steve wished they hadn't.

Steve looked behind again. Still he found no vehicles heading their way except for a tiny pair of headlights coming around a bend in the far lane. It posed no threat. The vehicle wouldn't be passing near the shoulder of the highway they were running on. Charlie's pace slowed down to that of a snapping turtle. He seemed desperate to stop, but also desperate to win.

He mumbled some words, but Steve was too busy thinking. What was the right thing to do? Should he stop chasing him? No, it was too late for that. Should he try to talk him out of it? Not really – the more he talked, the more daring Charlie would get. After all the years of dealing with him, Steve knew that much. Should he use force? But how? And when? They were in the middle of nowhere, for Christ's sake!

To think, Steve actually thought he was doing well up to this point. He even visualized Charlie succumbing to his wishes: after they ran a few more miles through trenches and valleys, Charlie would realize how much his little brother loved and cared for him and say, "Okay, you are right. Let's go home" and put his arm around Steve's shoulders and get in the vehicle, eating the grapes Jasmine had packed for him, and asking what's for dinner.

Instead, Charlie laid out an ultimatum, and Steve was reminded that he wasn't a gambler.

"I'm...serious. I'm...jumping...on...the...next car. You...just watch. I...am...jumping!" yelled Charlie, his voice strong and clear as if summoning up the courage to do what he claimed he would do. He looked back for any oncoming vehicles, and spotted only what Steve had already seen.

With the occasional vehicles zooming by from the other side, Steve's heart froze even more. Then, something made him turn back. This time, he saw a pair of headlights blazing directly towards them. The vehicle had switched lanes! His eyes widened and he almost tripped himself.

Charlie turned around, too, spotting the vehicle. His face turned ghostly white and his eyes narrowed into a deadly stare.

The vehicle sped towards them as the sound of screeching tires got louder and louder. Steve looked at Charlie, then at the vehicle, then at Charlie, then at the vehicle. The beaming headlights penetrated the gray world, demanding all the attention, creating long shadows that got shorter by the second.

"You...just watch...this!" Charlie shouted in a tone of finality, the sound of his voice rising above the screeching tires. The brilliant glare bounced off his sweat-glistened face, blue sweatshirt, gray pants, highlighting his conviction. He closed his eyes, tightened his jaw, braced his knees...!

Steve grabbed Charlie's waist from behind, and, using his own forward momentum, picked him up and swung him counterclockwise. Just then the blazing headlights whizzed by, missing them by no more than a few inches, followed by the sound of a blaring horn and the sweeping wind.

With the momentum of the first swing, Steve was able to spin Charlie around once to the right. By the third circular swing, which Steve couldn't control, he and Charlie were off the shoulder of the highway and on the steep slope on the side of the road. They tumbled freely, their bodies and limbs intertwined, snapping through wild bushes and dry plants.

CHAPTER THIRTEEN
the grapevine

No one moved. Steve wanted to lie there all night, comforted by the smell of the earth. He thought about how he used to wonder what these side plains off a highway were like every time he peered out a vehicle window. Now he finally had the chance to find out. Strangely, the word "real" came to his mind. It was real! The pictures that had reeled across his window so many times were indeed real. In fact, they were more real than the highway. The smell of the fresh clay, the sound of the crickets, the feel of the dry plants, and the open plain worked like a time machine, sending him back to his childhood, when life had been more real and more permanent. The only thing that wasn't real was growing up. Was life about falling into a sleep, falling into a dreamland? Why couldn't we stay a child forever?

"Get your hands off me, Motherfucker," yelled Charlie, snapping Steve back to reality. And – poof! Just like that, everything was gone, and Steve was back in a world where he was nothing more than a motherfucker.

Steve ached all over, but he didn't feel any sharp pains – nothing seemed broken. Charlie didn't seem to be in any major pain, either. Both of them had learned in martial arts how to break a fall, though Steve wasn't sure if he had applied his knowledge during their tumble.

"Let go!" yelled Charlie again. It was then that Steve realized he hadn't let go of Charlie's waist this whole time.

Charlie stood up quickly, escaping Steve's grip. He turned around, ready to climb back up the hill. Steve stood up and lunged at Charlie, again wrapping his hands around Charlie's waist from behind. Charlie tried to free himself, but Steve's hands were already locked together. With his feet planted behind Charlie's heels, Steve pulled Charlie down backwards, tripping Charlie's legs. They fell together hard. Charlie landed on his hands and knees before his entire body flopped to the ground. As soon as Steve's right side touched the ground, he kicked up his left leg high in the air, circled Charlie, and landed on top of him.

"Urgggggg," Charlie screamed, as the air went out of his lungs from the double impact of the ground and Steve's weight. Catching a few quick breaths, Charlie tried unsuccessfully to use the back of his neck to head butt Steve. He then threw some weak back fists to Steve's forehead and nose. Still holding Charlie with his right arm and supporting his own weight with the other, Steve moved off Charlie's back. Charlie stopped punching, got on his hands and knees to stand up. Steve had waited for this moment. When Charlie was on his knees, Steve wrapped his left leg around the outside of Charlie's thigh, curled over the inside of his calf and locked his foot around Charlie's ankle. As soon as Charlie tried to stand on his other leg, Steve wrapped it up with his right leg the same way he had with his left.

Their legs were wrapped like strands of a grapevine, which was in fact what the move was called. If Steve straightened out his legs, Charlie's would also straighten. It was an old wrestling move that Steve learned in high school. Not wasting any time, Steve straightened his knees, forcing Charlie's knees to straighten. With the weight of Steve's body on top of him, Charlie could only fall back to the ground.

"Fuck!" shouted Charlie. He reached behind him to grab hold of any part of Steve he could. Steve had hoped for this. As soon as Charlie exposed his flailing arms, Steve wrapped his left arm around Charlie's biceps, and did the same with his right arm. He secured his hold by interlocking his fingers together behind Charlie's back. A Double Chicken Wing, it was called, because Charlie's arms looked like chicken wings in the hold. The double Grapevine with the Double Chicken Wing was the most effective way to secure anyone on the ground. Once locked, the hold was so effective that it was illegal to use in high school wrestling for more than an allotted time.

With Charlie's arms and legs secured, Steve went after the last appendage Charlie could possibly move: his neck. He pressed his head into the back of Charlie's head, and sent his face into the dirt. Steve was confident that not even a crazy, drugged-out psycho twice Charlie's size could break this hold. It wasn't a matter of strength, but a matter of leverage.

One more thing worried Steve about Charlie, but he was prepared to deal with it. If Charlie tried anything foolish like biting his own tongue, Steve was prepared to introduce Charlie's jaw to yet another wrestling move: the cross face. He would wrap Charlie's face tightly with his left arm, stuffing his forearm into Charlie's mouth. Charlie could bite him, but at least he wouldn't be biting his own tongue. And if Steve shoved Charlie's mouth hard enough, Charlie wouldn't have the leverage to clamp down his jaw.

Once everything was secured, Steve tried to calm himself down and control his adrenaline. Endurance was the key to winning, his martial arts training told him. He must outlast Charlie. Actually, the whole ordeal had refreshed him. His mind and body felt as one again.

There was absolutely no turning back now – Oh, Steve knew that for sure.

"Let go, you Motherfucker! I don't fuckin' believe this. I don't fuckin' believe this shittttttt! I'm gonna fuckin' kill you, Motherfucker! I'm gonna fuckin' kill you! Ahrgggggggg!" shouted Charlie, on and on and on, occasionally spitting out the dirt he had eaten. He tried everything to free himself.

Steve was amazed that Charlie could still generate so much resistance. Just moments ago, he was about to collapse from exhaustion and could barely walk straight. But now, he was in a pure rage. There was so much anger in him, so much hate – or was it pride? – that his body seemed to work overtime to supply him with impressive, but dangerous, amounts of adrenaline. If so, then Charlie was about to crash. No one could produce that much adrenaline without paying a heavy price later on. He looked like a flopping fish, gasping for oxygen, fighting for his dear life. Steve wondered what that made him.

Nevertheless, Steve held on. There was only one way to beat Charlie's rage and that was to keep himself focused. He maneuvered his body to foil Charlie's escape attempts, using the pressure of his limbs and head to equalize his center of gravity. For every thousand volts of energy Charlie spent trying to free himself, Steve countered with a tenth of Charlie's effort. Eventually, after some monumental attempts, Charlie came to the realization that his situation was impossible and ceased his struggling, though he continued his hollering.

Charlie hollered with all the strength he could muster, his entire body tensing each and every time, until he couldn't holler anymore. In the end, his voice shrieked, but no sound came out. His neck muscles went limp and his head dug itself into the ground. Steve stopped pressing it. Charlie's body went limp as well. Although Steve continued to hold Charlie, he leaned slightly to his side to alleviate his weight from Charlie. Charlie let out a small yelp, as if the new position allowed him to breathe a little easier.

Eventually, everything became eerily peaceful. Even the freeway up on the hill brought no sound. Steve checked his surroundings for the first time. The tall, dry plants swayed and whistled to the faint breath of the summer night breeze. The crickets resumed their cries. Steve could smell the fresh clay. Everything looked normal, as if no one in this world cared about what was going on in the ditch of the famous Catherlina Beach Road. With the serenity came another dilemma. With his body still pinning Charlie to the ground, Steve wondered what he should do next.

Time passed.

Steve was almost drifting to sleep when he heard sounds of vehicle doors slamming. Then he heard faint voices. He contemplated how best to get their attention without spooking them, but Charlie was already ahead of him. With renewed strength,

Charlie resumed his yelling. This time he was calling for help, taking the word right out of Steve's mouth.

"Help! Help! Somebody help me, please! Help! Help!" yelled Charlie. Then he spoke to Steve. "You are now in trouble, Asshole. They'll arrest your ass."

Steve felt bad for Charlie. Charlie must be confused about who was really in trouble. Who was going to arrest whom?

"What's going on over there? Who's over there?" came the muffled sound of a man from the highway.

"Oh, fuck!" yelled Charlie and he yelled no more.

Steve wondered why, but then realized the man had spoken in Korean. It was the voice of Jang. How had he traced us – Had Charlie been that loud? In any case, Steve was relieved. He had forgotten about Jang and Benny.

Hearing Jang's voice brought Steve back to the present state. He realized how dreamy the whole affair of wrestling with Charlie had been.

Jang and Benny made their way to the ditch, tripping and sliding as they struggled to keep their balance down the steep hill.

Charlie spoke to Steve again. This time, he was pleading. "Let me go, Steve. Come on, let me go."

Steve knew why. Charlie didn't want Jang to see him this way. This was as degrading as he could imagine: Steve was manhandling him, pinning him to the ground, accusing him of being a loser. Jang and Benny would witness the whole thing and would acknowledge his pitiful status. The great Charlie Lee, the natural-born leader, the king of the jungle, accused of being a drug addict, a lunatic, a wrecker of his own family. Charlie couldn't let Jang see him this way. Not because he didn't want to be accused, but because he might see himself through Jang's eyes.

Nevertheless, Steve didn't let Charlie go. It wasn't the right time. He needed more time to think through all the angles. He apologized to Charlie a thousand times inside, but pity didn't solve problems. Truth did.

"What...what's going on here?" asked Jang, startled by what he saw: his two sons flat on the ground, cuts and bruises all over their bodies and dirt-covered faces, their hair full of wild debris, their clothing ripped, and their eyes reflecting the fire of Hell.

Benny, who was behind Jang, summed up their collective opinion:

"Shit," he murmured.

"What the Hell is going on here?!" yelled Jang, again.

Charlie's body became rigid, like a worm on a hook.

"Let me go, you Motherfucker!" said Charlie to Steve.

"Hey, what's the matter with you? Your little brother wants to take you home," yelled Jang, rivaling Charlie's volume.

"Let me go, Steve. I mean it this time. Let me go."

Charlie's pleas were so heart wrenching, so effective, that Steve had to harden his heart to continue holding him.

"I don't believe what I am seeing!" said Jang. "Hey, don't you know where you are? Don't you know what you are doing right now?"

"Leave me the fuck alone! I don't need you or anyone else. Just get the fuck away from me!"

"What? Don't you speak to me with that kind of language. Don't you know who I am?"

"I don't give a shit who you are. Just leave me alone!"

"What, what did you say? I can't believe what I'm hearing. Is this what America has taught you? Don't you disrespect me this way. This is the most ridiculous...."

"Fuck you! Fuck all of you. Just leave me the fuck alone! Everyone just get the fuck out of my life!"

"Okay fine, then let's end this here. I can't take anymore of this. Let's all just end this now for good."

Jang took a couple of steps forward and swung his foot into Charlie's face. Charlie dodged the kick but winced as it landed on his shoulder instead. The dry plant debris kicked up in the air forming a tiny cloud of dust, enough to irritate both Steve's and Charlie's eyes. Jang stumbled backward from his own kick, losing his balance. Benny supported him.

"Dad, stop it! Stop!" said Steve, exasperated. He wasn't holding Charlie so Jang could have a free whack at him. Steve let Charlie's right arm go so he could stop Jang, who was positioning to kick Charlie again. Charlie quickly used his freed arm to stand up. He then freed his left arm of Steve, who was busy trying to stop Jang's attempt to kick again.

Benny intervened and held Jang. Charlie stood halfway up, with both his hands and feet touching the ground. Steve still lay on top of him, their legs wrapped around each other. Charlie couldn't stand any higher with Steve's weight on him and his legs wrapped. Instead, he lifted his hips high and lowered his head, shaking Steve loose by sliding him forward. He was instinctively making the right move to escape the grapevine. One of the most effective ways to escape the hold was to stand on all fours and let the person in the back slide forward. Steve's legs no longer wrapped Charlie's. Instead, they were around Charlie's waist. Steve had to support his sliding body by putting his hands on the ground and changing his leg position to the Figure Four Leg Lock, which squeezed Charlie's waist and prevented him from sliding further.

They stayed in that position for what seemed like an eternity. Realizing that Steve was no longer sliding down his back, and tired from carrying his weight, Charlie fell sideways, hoping to land on his back and squash Steve into the ground. It was a mistake Steve had hoped Charlie would make. As soon as Charlie fell to his side, Steve quickly rewrapped Charlie's arms into Double Chicken Wings. Charlie fought harder this time, but he couldn't counter a move he didn't know. He succeeded in rolling his body backward, but Steve's Figure Four Leg Lock prevented him from moving any further. Charlie kicked wildly in the air, like a snapping turtle on its back. Steve waited until Charlie stopped kicking and then rewrapped Charlie's legs into the Grapevine. Even though Steve was on the ground with Charlie lying on top of him, Charlie was once again locked in and couldn't move his limbs. After resting a few seconds to gather his strength, Steve swung Charlie to his left, the circular momentum allowing him to once again roll Charlie to the ground with him on top.

Benny struggled to keep Jang in check. He didn't want to be disrespectful and wasn't sure how much force was appropriate to contain Jang. He knew the Lee family took their Asian customs seriously – elders were to be respected at all times. Benny still saw himself as a kid to Jang. When Jang yelled at Benny about how dare he hold him like that, Benny became flustered and reluctantly let him go. Though Jang spoke to Benny in Korean and Benny couldn't understand the language, the tone of his voice was more than enough to make Benny panic.

Wasting no time, Jang planted a vicious kick in Charlie's face. This one hit hard, making a loud tweaking sound against Charlie's open jaw. The pain reached all the way into Steve's heart.

"Jesus Christ, Dad, wha...what are you doing? Oh my God!" said Steve.

"It's over. It's all over," said Jang, preparing for another kick. His face wore the expression of a man who had lost everything.

Steve freed his hands again, and even one of his legs to stop him from stomping on Charlie's face. Jang lifted his knee, ready to squash Charlie's face in the ground. Steve covered Charlie's face with his left arm and grabbed Jang's foot with his right.

"Let go! Let go! Let me kill him!" yelled Jang.

"Stop, Dad, stop!" yelled Steve.

"Will you let go? Leave it! Let go! Damn it!" yelled Jang.

Jang twisted Steve's hands by wrapping his foot around Steve's wrist and twisting it free. He moved swiftly towards Charlie. He was ready to dig his hard-soled heel into Charlie's face. This time, Steve had to practically let Charlie go to stop Jang. He was desperate, torn between what to let go, what to hold on to, who to stop, who to protect.

This time, Steve told Benny to get involved, to grow up.

"Benny, hold him!" yelled Steve.

As if on cue, Benny moved with more authority. Just as Jang freed himself from Steve's grip for the second time, Benny grabbed his waist, picked him up, and took a few steps back. Charlie tried to escape, even stood up, but Steve held him down again.

"Let me go. I'm gonna finish this. We'll all end here, today. I can't go on like this," said Jang.

His limbs kicked and punched in the air like he was a human caterpillar.

Steve realized then that bringing Jang had doubled his problem. Why hadn't he thought of this before? You can't send an addict to bring an addict home! Although Jang had never been a drug addict, he was an addict of a different sort. Charlie's addiction started only a few months ago, but Jang had been delusional for as long as Steve could remember. Addiction came in all forms.

Benny still seemed unsure about holding onto Jang, who was yelling at him in full blasts of Korean.

"Benny, you keep him there. Don't let him go. Forget what my Dad says," said Steve. Then he turned to Jang, "Dad, stop. Just stop."

"I'll stop at nothing. He needs to go to Hell with me. We all need to go. Is this what America has taught you? I don't want to live anymore! Let me go! Let me go!" yelled Jang.

"Fuckin' shit! Fuck you! Fuck you all! Kill me! Go ahead and kill me. Fuck you all!" yelled Charlie, on and on and on.

"Dad, we agreed not to do this, remember?" asked Steve, pleading.

"In all the years I've lived, this is one of the saddest times of my life. What did I ever do to deserve this? I just don't want to live like this anymore. Let me go. He needs to die with me! Let's all just die!"

As usual, Jang was passionate at the wrong time. He was in a world of make believe, as though millions were watching him and sympathizing with him. He needed to set aside his pride and concentrate on keeping his eldest son from destroying his life. He needed to think about everyone else. His choice of words, his actions, his tone of voice were too similar to those of the characters in the Korean TV soaps he watched.

"Shit! Fuck! Motherfucker!" Charlie yelled with every ounce of strength he could muster. It was anger from watching Jasmine suffer Jang's fury for years, anger at himself for not being able to do anything about it, anger that had finally made him run away. In a short time, Charlie could reach the point of no return, a point where his guilt and compassion would no longer play a part in his wanting to come home. Or anywhere else for that matter.

Steve tried to maintain his focus and keep his adrenaline in check. He needed to hold on. He needed to outlast everyone here. He needed to outlast the strength of the drugs. He couldn't give up. Just couldn't.

CHAPTER FOURTEEN
the hero

The Lee family lived next to a levee before they immigrated to America. The government built the levee to control the frequent flooding from the western mountains. The diameter of the elliptical levee reached a good two miles before the east end extended to the Han River, one of the major rivers in Korea. The east end consisted of many bridges that connected fast-developing highways in the reform-conscious country after the war. The base of the levee was surrounded by homes and businesses bustling with townspeople, all working hard to cash in on the resurging economy.

The levee stood fifty feet tall and was made of clay. The top was wide enough to have a small road and side trails on each end. Due to its gradual slope, even the middle of the levee had trails. Houses, businesses, roads, and everything else were located at the bottom of the levee. Although the levee's main function was to control the frequent floods in the region, it also served as an unofficial recreational park for the locals, many of whom lived in single rooms with shared outhouses and water stations. No one wanted to stay inside their space any longer than they had to, so the main street was always busy and noisy, especially from the street vendors. They wheeled their carts or carried Chige (Korean traditional back-carrier) on their backs and yelled at the top of their lungs to attract attention:

"Poooooooppppppp, pop, popcorn! Oh fun, pop, popcorn!..."

" Corn, dogidogidogidogi here, Corn dogidogidogidogi!..."

"Watermelon! Fresh watermelon! Watermelon! Fresh watermelon!..."

"Ice cream! Ice cream!..."

" Rice cakes, Rice cakes, love that sweet take! Rice cakes, Rice cakes..."

"American clothes, authentic American clothes! American

clothes..."

"Silk, yo, silk! Silk, yo, silk!..."

"Reddabada bean soups! Reddabada bean soups!..."

Crowds gathered around these vendors, blocking the roads and wreaking havoc as they bargained for better deals. Everything could be bargained: mothers bargained for clothes, kids bargained for toys, fathers bargained for radios, grandfathers and grandmothers bargained for rice and everything else. It was like the street fairs of New York City, only without the safety of police supervision and well-groomed crowds with fancy clothes and fat wallets.

The inside of the levee was usually dry, except for the tiny pond everyone called Han, mimicking the famous river. Technically, no one was supposed to be in the levee, but on any given day, people could be seen playing, crossing to the other side, transporting goods, finding edible plants, or swimming in the Han pond. The levee was always full of life.

The city of Hangikdong, one of the major cities in the Youngdongpo district, was located on the south side of the levee where the Lee family lived. The north side of the levee was inhabited by the lowest of the poverty-stricken, who endured unspeakably difficult living conditions and high crime rates. The city police didn't extend their services there very often, if at all. The lives of the people on the north side weren't regarded as important to the rest of civilization, despite the fact that many were victims of the war and some were even heroic veterans. In the event of a major flood, the city officials had an approved agenda to blow up the north side of the wall to let the water out in that direction. That would've resulted in more casualties, but so goes the history of civilization between the haves and have-nots.

Kids in the village spent much of their childhood catching wildlife around the levee wall. Finding a rare species was a trophy. Frogs were always fun to catch and play with, especially the fat ones. Lizards were special. Only the older kids were able to catch those and when they did, they would charge admission fees to let the younger kids see them. The excited kids would gather around with their coins and be awed at the sight of the beautiful lizard sticking its tongue out like a laser beam from a spaceship. It was worth every cent every time.

Butterflies were a popular catch, too. Kids even traded them, often using them for school projects. Once, Young Steve couldn't believe his eyes when he saw a butterfly with a Yin-Yang symbol on both of its wings – part of the Korean flag! He got so nervous trying to catch it that he stumbled and could only watch the patriotic butterfly disappear. While the wildlife in the levee entertained the local kids, mothers searched frequently for edible plants. In certain seasons, tasty roots like the delicacy Dorajie (Bellflower roots) could be found inside the levee. Mothers would turn over the ground looking for them, inadvertently preparing the ground for new crops for the following year. Teenagers spent their time on the small Han pond swimming, catching fish, or making waves. Sometimes leeches stuck to them like bad acne, but no one cared any more than they cared about the frequent dog poop that littered the streets. Fathers spent their time on the top of the hill gambling with Yutnori, a traditional Korean game, and drinking bowls of Makgoli, a home-made rice wine. Grandfathers and grandmothers strolled on the top of the levee to enjoy the cool breeze and to enhance their digestion. It was customary to pay them respect and offer them samples of food. The elders were always included in the busy scenes of the levee neighborhood. Mosquitoes prevented everyone from staying out late, but sometimes people ended up doing so anyway and caught glimpses of sparkling fireflies or the bright moon. The lack of electricity in the village only enhanced the beauty of the nights.

Winters were just as fun as summers as the Han pond became a skating rink. Many people didn't have proper skates, so they used thin strips of tree bark under their shoes. The slopes of the levee served as trails for sledding, or a battleground for massive snowball fights. Street vendors still roamed the main street, making them perfect targets for the snowball snipers. Of course, these vendors were the original snipers, so when some of them retaliated, the snowball fights between the old and the new were entertaining enough for everyone to watch. The kids made many snowmen, but the clay ground didn't allow them to make white snowmen like they had seen in comic books. To them, a pure white snowman was as real as Santa Claus. Nevertheless, on snowy days gray snowmen of every shape stood proudly all around the levee, only to be "executed" by rogue kids during the night. The rogue kids destroyed these snowmen by punching, kicking, and tackling them, imagining themselves as Muhammad Ali or Bruce Lee. Very few snowmen ended up standing for more than a day or so. Ali will never know how many more men he knocked down during his career.

Everyone knew each other. Friendships and family ties were strong. Sometimes, friends and families were all they had to put food on their table for the day. Life around the village was harsh, but not without rewards. The ever-present specter of death and starvation caused them to embrace and appreciate life and happiness even more. Compassion was easily found. Heroes and miracles could be seen every day: friends helped friends in need, babies suckled milk from different mothers, townspeople gathered together to protect their own, younglings were constantly supervised and educated by random elders. The circle of life was evident. No one questioned it.

One glorious Saturday afternoon, Charlie and Steve were catching dragonflies at the top of the levee when two boys confronted Charlie about his skipping classes at school. Schools operated six days a week back then and included a half-day on Saturday. It wasn't unusual that a few popular kids like Charlie would sometimes skip Saturdays on purpose just to tempt fate. The consequence of skipping classes was brutal if teachers ever found out. Charlie wanted his followers to know that he wasn't afraid of authority. Sometimes, the followers got punished for Charlie's skipping instead of Charlie, but they didn't care. They would gladly take their punishments for their MIA leader. But not all of them did.

"We got in trouble because of you, Charlie Lee," said one of the boys.

"Yeah, man, we had to stay after and clean the classroom and the stairways," said the other. They didn't look happy.

Charlie ignored their comments and continued to concentrate on finding a dragonfly. He had just bought a small chick from a schoolyard and wanted to see it eat a live dragonfly.

"Hey, I'm talking to you, Charlie Lee," said the first boy. Usually, the kids at school called each other by their full names because that's what they were accustomed to hearing during the daily attendance call taken by the homeroom teachers.

"Yeah, he's talking to you. You better listen if you know what's good for ya," said the other, obviously a sidekick to the first boy.

This wasn't good, Steve thought. If the first boy had a sidekick, he must be someone really tough. Only the tough kids had an entourage.

"It's none of your business. Why don't you butt out?!" said Charlie.

"What? What did you say? Are you talking to me?" said First Boy, who turned to face his sidekick, acting appalled. "Is he talking to me?"

"Shit, man, I think he is talking to you, man," answered Sidekick, getting charged up.

"You better shut your mouth, little kid, or I may have to readjust it," said First Boy, looking back at Charlie.

Charlie was ready to shout back, but young Steve pulled on his shirt.

"Charlie, be quiet. They look really mad."

Charlie looked at Steve and patted his shoulder.

"Don't worry, Steve, they aren't going to do anything." Then he shouted to the boys, "Just go on home, and leave me alone.

I don't want to bother with you."

"Well, I want to bother you, Sucker. I'm tired of the bullshit you pull on Saturdays. I don't think you are tough. I think you're all talk. In fact, I'm ready to prove it," said First Boy.

"Oh, man, you better watch out, Charlie Lee. We gonna getcha," said Sidekick.

Steve was so scared he didn't know what to do. He thought about running home and bringing his mother back, or at least some of Charlie's loyal followers, but no one was around except for a few kids who would rather see Charlie in action than fight alongside him. So Steve kept pulling on Charlie's shirt.

"Charlie, let's go home. I'm scared. Please, let's go home," said Steve.

"It's okay, Steve. Let go of my shirt," said Charlie.

The tough boys read Charlie's hesitation. First Boy shouted, "You stay where you are. I'm coming over there to kick your ass!" He dropped his schoolbag and ran over to Charlie.

"Yeah, man, you stay there. We'll kick your ass!" said Sidekick, doing the same.

Steve panicked. These were the boys from the other side of the village, the North side – a place he was forbidden to even look at. These kids didn't bluff – when they told you they would beat you up, they *would* beat you up. Steve heard rumors about how lawlessness ran amok there, and how kids fought every day just for fun. Some even carried switchblades. He heard that most of the people there had committed at least one murder by the time they reached their teens.

Charlie didn't move. Instead, he calmly watched as the two kids came after him, seemingly more agitated about not being able to concentrate on catching dragonflies than about having to fight the two killers. He was so relaxed he almost looked bored, as if he was ready to take a nap. First Boy positioned himself in front of Charlie and Sidekick stood behind him. They ignored little Steve, who was busy trying to hide nearby.

Then, without warning, First Boy swung at Charlie with his left hand. Charlie blocked it with his right hand. First Boy then swung his right, even stronger and wider than his previous attack, as if that had been a decoy. Charlie ducked and First Boy's body twisted out of control as he missed his target and started to fall to the ground. Charlie unleashed a perfectly-timed-left uppercut on the falling boy's ribs, followed by a right hook that landed squarely on his jaw. Charlie's moves were precise and maximized for power as he pivoted his hips and locked his shoulder. Within a split second, the menacing boy dropped to the ground. Sidekick, shocked by Charlie's ferocity, didn't move a muscle. Charlie turned around and gave him a straight left back kick to his stomach. The boy let out a huge gasp and doubled-over onto his knees. Before Steve could comprehend what was happening, Charlie had demolished the two devils from Hell. Steve was ready to leap into the air and cheer for his hero. But not before he knew for sure that it was safe for him to come out of hiding.

"Now what you gonna say, huh?!" mocked Charlie.

The two boys only groaned in pain.

"Hold on, now I'm really gonna kick your ass," said Charlie, clenching his fists again.

The two boys got to their knees, and, with their hands together, pleaded with Charlie for mercy.

"Oh, Charlie Lee, I'm sorry for what I said. Please forgive me. Oh, please. You can be absent any Saturdays you want, Charlie Lee. Please," said First Boy, crying. Two of his teeth were missing.

"Yeah, me too," said Sidekick, crying twice as loud because of the pain in his stomach and his duty to echo his friend's words.

Steve couldn't believe his eyes. Charlie seemed ten feet tall! Charlie barked something at them again and the two boys ran away as fast as they could, their papers and pencils popping out of their pockets, the cracks of their butts showing in their baggy pants. Steve and Charlie watched with satisfaction as the boys kept running even after they reached the top of the other side of the levee.

Many kids who saw the fight were already talking loudly among themselves. The news would surely travel fast. Charlie would be even more popular, if that was even possible. He probably wouldn't have to go to school anymore. Steve was in awe of the hero that stood in front of him. His brother – his very own brother, Mr. Charlie Lee – was the Knight in Shining Armor.

"Wow, Charlie, you were amazing!"

"What? This?" Charlie smiled.

"You...you beat those big kids really good! Wow!"

"Heh, heh, I was good, wasn't I?"

"How did you duck so fast? I couldn't even see!"

"I don't know. It just happened. I didn't plan it."

"And that punch after the duck. That was so, so cool!"

"Oh yeah, that was cool, wasn't it?" Charlie was getting excited, as if he just realized what he had done. This only made Steve more jumpy. How could Charlie not know until now what he had done? Charlie seemed so modest. So, so, cool.

"Charlie, you look like a movie star, a Bruce Lee," said Steve, star struck.

"It's no big deal. If they come back again, I'll really kick their asses," said Charlie, throwing some punches in the air.

Little Steve couldn't put Charlie's amazing moves out of his mind: the technique, the precision, the triumph. He saw that size did not matter in a fight, only knowledge and courage. The more he thought about it, the better it got. Steve couldn't contain himself. He realized it was possible for a little guy to stand up to a bigger guy. Two bigger guys. Were there more moves like those out there? Could someone like him learn them? Could he, if he worked hard, be a hero like Charlie? In the summer of '72, little Steve was full of dreams. The path to the world of martial arts slowly revealed itself to him. It would change the course of his life.

CHAPTER FIFTEEN
the compromise

Charlie mentioned a word that caused a light bulb to go off in Steve's head. Eureka! An alternative solution! Why didn't he think of that?!

"Pretty soon the cops are gonna crawl all over here. They'll lock your ass up for this. You watch. I ain't kiddin'," said Charlie.

Steve finally realized what Charlie meant when he kept making threats about "getting in trouble for this." It had never occurred to Steve that he may be committing an illegal act: harassing someone or maybe even kidnapping! But that didn't matter. The sight of police would be good. If he were going to get locked up, then Charlie would get locked up, too. If he couldn't bring Charlie home, then jail would be the next best option. Perhaps spending the night in jail might even be good for Charlie. Maybe being locked up in a grimy cell overnight would bring Charlie to his senses.

Involving a third party, however, especially the police, could result in today's fiasco leaking out into the Korean community. The gossip would be too juicy for any of them to ignore. With the jail time involved, Steve and Charlie would be the hot topic of every Korean's conversation on this side of the Mississippi.

"That's fine with me, man. If you aren't going home with me, I'll be happy to go to the police with you," said Steve.

"Good, Asshole. Why don't we go there now? You'll be locked up in a minute."

"You want to go now? Lead the way, man. Let's go. I'm not afraid of the police."

"Good. Let's all go to the police. I hope they lock you up and throw away the keys!" Jang shouted.

Steve let go of Charlie. Charlie seemed in no mood to run again as he was barely able to stand up, but if he did, Steve would simply catch him and secure him. Besides, Charlie wouldn't conjure up a plan to go to the police if he thought he could still escape from Steve. Benny let go of Jang. Almost on cue, all four of them started dusting themselves off. Just moments ago, Jang and Charlie had been ready to kill each other, but now they looked as if they had just gotten up from a night's rest in a hay barn. Everyone looked calm again. No one talked. One by one, they walked up the slope. Steve stayed close to Charlie.

"I ain't riding with Dad," said Charlie.

"Fine," said Steve. Who could blame him?

"Benny, mang, we'll go together," said Charlie, as the group reached the top.

Benny's face changed. What if Charlie went nuts and grabbed the steering wheel, swerving the car off a cliff in some kind of suicide attempt? Or broke a window and jumped out? After seeing how Charlie had behaved, Benny knew that anything was possible. Still, though, Benny did his best to hide his fears and offered his friendship to Charlie.

"All right, mang. Get in the car. Let me just clean some shit outta there."

"Dad, you just follow us. I'll go in the backseat with Charlie," said Steve.

Charlie frowned.

"I ain't riding with you. You go with Dad," said Charlie.

"I am riding with you. It's either that or we all go in Dad's car."

"Fuck you. Go with Dad."

"I ain't going anywhere unless we ride together."

After some long sighs, and some more swearing, Charlie climbed in.

Steve walked over to Jang who was already in his vehicle, lighting his cigarette and buckling the seatbelt. He fumbled the cigarette as it bounced off his lap and onto the floor. The belt buckle recoiled and hit his nose. "God damn!" he spoke under his breath as he searched for the cigarette. By the time he retrieved it and tried to light it, the lighter had lost its heat. "Christ," he spoke under his breath again, as he pushed in the lighter button for the second time.

"Dad, you should go home," said Steve.

"I'm not going home."

"I think it's best for all of us if you go home. There's nothing you can do once we're at the police station," said Steve, avoiding the word "jail."

"I said I'm not going home, for crying out loud!"

Steve didn't push the subject any further. He knew how to handle him: don't mind him and don't rely on him. Maybe if Jasmine had handled him this way, she would've been better off by now. Steve also wanted to tell Jang to control his temper, but he didn't. For now, Jang seemed fine as long as he had his cigarettes.

As Steve went back to Benny's Camaro, he noticed Benny wasn't in the vehicle. Charlie was sitting in the front seat. Oh great, Steve thought. Benny stood by the driver's side door, waiting for Steve to do something. Steve was in no mood to be patient this time. This was nonsense. Charlie was challenging Steve's every move.

"Yo, bro, you should ride in the back," said Steve, mindful of being non-confrontational.

"Fuck you. I'm riding in the front. You go ride with Dad."

"Then we ain't going anywhere. We'll just wait here all night until the police arrive."

Charlie didn't reply.

"We can wait here all night. I ain't going anywhere. Benny ain't gonna drive until you get in the back anyway," said Steve

"Yo, Benny, get in the car and drive," said Charlie.

"Hey, mang, I think you should do what your brother said," said Benny.

"Will you get in the fuckin' car and drive? What the fuck is the matter with you?" shouted Charlie.

"Yo, Charlie, mang...."

"If you want to end this fast," said Steve, cutting Benny off, "then just get in the back." He didn't want Benny to take more heat. "You're the one who wanted to go to the police, why are you making it so difficult?"

"Benny, drive!" Charlie shouted, ignoring Steve.

Benny didn't reply. There was an awkward silence. Finally, with another huge sigh and some motherfuckin' this and motherfuckin' that, Charlie climbed into the back. Steve lowered his head to get in next to him.

"Don't you fuckin' come in here," said Charlie.

Steve climbed in anyway, locking the front passenger door after him. Benny got in. Without saying a word, Steve reached across Charlie and locked the driver side door as well. Luckily, the Camaro was a two-door coupe. Charlie wouldn't be able to jump out unless he moved to the front seat first.

"Benny, can you turn on the interior light for the trip?" asked Steve, letting Charlie know that he would be watching him very closely.

"Sure, mang," said Benny, as he started up the vehicle. The crank sounded unusually shaky under the thin backseat.

For a moment, Steve saw flashes of their lives in the middle of a high-speed car wreck, like teenage drunk drivers during their high school proms. If something did happen to them during the ride, Jasmine would be missing two sons and Benny's family would be missing one. At least Steve could control Charlie outside, but inside the speeding vehicle, one bad move could result in dire consequences for both families. The night wasn't over yet. Not by a long shot.

CHAPTER SIXTEEN
the talk

Steve frequently checked his rearview for Jang, who was doing a good job of following them while still giving them some space. Maybe Jang anticipated a body being tossed out of Benny's vehicle. Steve was glad that Jang hadn't gone home. If anything happened on the highway, Jang could block oncoming traffic for them, or if Charlie happened to take control of the wheel, Jang could chase him.

Jang's single most valuable contribution to the Lee family was his driving. Jasmine didn't know how to drive, so Jang drove her to work, grocery shopping, weekend errands, and special functions. Though he complained a lot, Jang enjoyed his chauffeur duties. Driving was the one thing he could do that his wife couldn't. When Jasmine wanted to learn how to drive, he volunteered to teach her, thereby legitimizing his complaints, and purposely made driving seem more difficult than it really was. At the same time, he was extra nice to her while chauffeuring, so she ended up ditching the idea. Without his driving services, Jang truly had no control over his family.

The ride to the police station wasn't as dangerous as Steve had feared. Although Charlie didn't behave well inside the vehicle, he wasn't suicidal. Charlie screamed a lot and sometimes punched Steve, but they were only expressions of frustration. Charlie was too weak and too worn out to pack any power in his punches, and even if he weren't, he didn't have enough space to wind up his swings or set his positions properly.

Benny drove quietly, with his seatbelt secured tightly and his hands firmly on the steering wheel. He cruised at fifty miles per hour, staying in the slow lane. He didn't dare open his mouth. Occasionally, Charlie gave him directions to the police station and Benny followed them, throwing in the homie word "mang" to alleviate the tension that had built up between them. In time, Charlie's voice became friendlier towards him. After all, Benny didn't have to do all this, and Charlie knew that. They went way back.

Eventually, Charlie settled down enough for Steve to relax a bit. Steve could feel his adrenaline slowly leaving him. He fought hard to keep it. He needed to maintain his strength until the end. He had seen many times during his martial arts training how fighters lost towards the end of a match because they relaxed prematurely. It was never over until it was over. The night seemed like it was about to fold soon, but it wasn't over yet. He still had to deal with the police, and Charlie might still act up and punch him some more. The worst might be yet to come, he thought. He had to stay alert.

The whole ride reminded him of his childhood when he had to wait his turn for a beating from Jasmine while she finished punishing Charlie first. Now, he was waiting to take the beating from Charlie himself. Since Jang had also beaten him before, he mused that Kimberly was the last family member who needed to beat his ass to complete the cycle. Who knows? She does have that mean streak. He chuckled at the silly thought and closed his eyes. Everything that happened today seemed so unreal, as though he would soon wake up and find that it was all a dream. Just to amuse himself, he opened his eyes halfway and closed them again. *"Guess not."* The momentary opening and closing of his eyes only made him sleepier. The steady humming of the engine didn't help either. He opened his eyes wide, took a deep breath, and sat up straight. He cursed himself for his momentary lack of focus and cleared his throat. He had to stay alert.

He wondered what it would be like to sleep in jail. Would the police understand his situation? What about the thugs he might be locked up with? Some of the prisoners he saw on TV looked very intimidating. They were big and nasty looking with goatees and tattoos, like the two Harley Davidson thugs he met back at the beach. They also carried weapons, inconspicuously hidden on their bodies. Then there was that rape thing people talked about. Could it happen to a person in an overnight jail? Steve's butt cheeks twitched.

The Korean neighbors would have a field day when they hear about Steve's and Charlie's arrests. Steve, the good son, heading to jail...with his butt cheeks twitching. He could almost see the smirks on their faces. But he worried about Jasmine the most. Without a clue as to what was happening to them right now, she would be expecting them at any moment, carefully rearranging her hot meal so that it would stay warm as long as possible. How would she take the news? Or could she? Steve's heart sank again. There was so much to do and so little time.

From the appearance of more streetlights, Steve sensed they were nearing the police station. He could see Charlie more clearly. Charlie's eyes were wide open again and he seemed apprehensive. In fact, he seemed to become more restless by the second, fidgeting erratically. His hair was so greasy that it formed to the shape of the grip wherever he touched it. It was time for another eruption.

"They'll lock you up. You can't do this to someone," said Charlie, his voice hoarse from yelling all day. He was so weak that even breathing strained him.

Steve didn't reply.

"Hurry up Benny, I want to see this asshole get locked up," said Charlie, disappointed by Steve's lack of response. "This is the stupidest night I've ever had. I could be in my own home watching a movie right now. I don't fuckin' believe this! What did I ever do to you?"

Charlie spoke with lots of bluster in his words, like those people in church who periodically blurted out "Amen!" every time the minister uttered a good line. An entire lung full of air, just for one word. The ultimate declaration of conviction, but spoken with an over exaggeration that betrayed their hidden doubts. Charlie's "What did I ever do to you?" was his "Amen!"

"I don't know what the fuck your problem is. Why don't

you just leave me alone?" yelled Charlie, getting so charged up by the loudness of his own voice that he was on the verge of hyperventilating. There were two ways to deal a mistake: one was to fix it and the other was to go with it. Charlie never had the courage to fix it, so he always went with it.

More punches came in Steve's direction, but he blocked most of them. Benny swerved his vehicle a little.

Steve maintained his silence. He was prepared to show Charlie the one thing Charlie never learned while growing up – actions spoke louder than words. He would do what he said he would do: they were going either to the police station or home but nowhere else.

"Why don't you just get out of my life," said Charlie. "Do you know why I'm doing this, Asshole? Do you know why I'm doing this? I'll tell you why. I'll tell you."

Charlie held his breath for a moment. Steve knew the next words he heard, he would never forget for the rest of his life.

"It's because of you," said Charlie.

With his defiant little brother next to him and with his best friend driving him to a police station, Charlie finally confronted his demons.

"Wha...?" Steve was about to reply.

"You fucked up my life."

"What are you talking about?"

"I hate you. You are the one who did this to me. All I want is for you to get the fuck out of my life. Over and done. I don't ever want to see your fuckin' face again! I can't believe you're here, bugging me like this. You live your life. I'll live mine. Just leave me alone."

Charlie quit on everything. He wanted to succeed but lacked dedication. He was brilliant at everything but specialized in nothing. He was his own worst enemy because he had vision but lacked conviction. As a child, he wanted to have more marbles than anyone on the whole block and he would always find ways to get more, only to lose even more. Jasmine suffered constantly from bailing him out. As a teenager, he wanted to have a good report card. He copied the homework and cheated on his tests to bring home a perfect report card only to fail miserably later on.

Then Charlie discovered girls.

Charlie's first serious girlfriend was Lola, whom he met during his senior year in high school. She was a compulsive liar. He soon fell into her spell and learned the darker side of life. Not that Charlie didn't know how to lie before, but he still felt guilty about it. Lola taught him otherwise. She could lie without batting an eye.

"She could lie and you'd never know, Steve," Charlie once told Steve, "I can never believe anything she says. I'll bet she can probably beat the lie detector test."

Charlie was proud of that fact.

"I think she's also a kleptomaniac," said Charlie.

"What's a kleptomaniac?" asked Steve.

"Oh, that's when somebody can't help themselves from stealing something. That chick is a compulsive liar and a kleptomaniac. I always have to watch out for her. You can never trust her with anything."

"Then, why are you with her?"

"I don't know. She's always tagging me, I guess. She can be cool sometimes, I guess."

From Lola, Charlie acquired the seed of ultimate failure: lying to himself. It was the beginning of the sickness for Charlie. Maybe the seed was already within him before he met Lola, but who could say for sure? Charlie's was nourished, nurtured and cared for by his first love.

As an adult, Charlie wanted money. His motivation for it was noble at first. He wanted to help out his family. Predictably, however, the allure of money, the lust for power, the limitlessness of greed, took the best of him. Money was his ultimate temptation, his ultimate foe. He lied, cheated, and hustled his way into a mountain of debt. Everyone in the family suffered from his mistakes – especially Jasmine. Charlie knew he screwed up, but he chose to run from them. He wanted to start over again, but he didn't have the courage to face his past. He wasn't strong enough. He was stuck. At twenty-four, he felt there were no more chances left for him, so he tried to kill himself slowly with drugs. But he couldn't do that completely either. The shadow of Jasmine always stopped him from sinking to the bottom of the ocean. He loved her that much. He loved her more than he hated himself. In fact, it was because he loved her so much that he got into all this trouble. Although she never pressured him for anything, her immense love was pressure enough – the pressure to be the perfect son. She deserved the perfect son. She deserved happiness. She deserved the happiness of having the perfect son.

It didn't help to see that his younger brother succeeded at everything he failed at. From the very beginning, Steve was different from him: always careful, always planning, and always playing by the rules. The more Steve succeeded, the more Charlie felt his failure. Steve's strong connection to the family only made Charlie feel more out of place. According to Korean tradition, Charlie as the first-born son was the rightful heir of the Lee family. But Charlie felt like his family didn't need him anymore. To them, he was a thorn in their eyes. Charlie felt abandoned, with no place to go and no one to blame. He lost the most important thing in his life. It wasn't the marbles. It wasn't the girls. It wasn't the money. It was something he thought he could never lose. He lost his family.

Steve could sense all that now. It was in Charlie's eyes. It was in Charlie's voice. But, instead of feeling compassion, he felt anger. In fact, when Charlie blamed him for everything, Steve's heart was ready to explode. The blatant accusations from Charlie hurt him more than any punch Charlie had thrown that evening because his words had come not from the drugs, but from his heart. They were words that had been locked up for a long time. How could Charlie not understand *his* position? Steve didn't mean to make Charlie feel bad by being the good son. Of all people, Charlie should've known that! Charlie had to know that sometimes it was just as difficult to work hard to achieve success as it was to suffer from failure. The pressure of not making a mistake was just as hard as making one and living with it.

"I can't believe you're bugging *me*," Steve replied. He was through taking it. Who was bugging whom?

"It's you. God damn it. I hate you. You are the one who did this to me."

"How can this be my fault?"

"I didn't come home because I knew you would be there for the summer. I would've come home after you left. You're the reason why I wasn't coming home."

"Don't blame this on me. I never did anything to hurt you."

"You did, Asshole, more than you know. You and your goody two-shoes attitude. You think you can change the world, don't you? You're the reason why I quit school. You're the reason why I started this shit. You think you can come around here every time you have a break and fix everything and then go away? You think life is that easy? I'm the one who stayed with the family when you were away. I'm the one who took care of them. You don't know half the shit you think you know."

"What do you mean you took care of them?"

"I'm the one who was with them. I'm the one who took care of their everyday shit. As much as you'd like to think differently, without me, they wouldn't be able to do jack. You fuckin' come here once every blue moon and think you're the one who sets everything straight. What the fuck do you think you did that was so important? Were you there when Mom needed to put in a new septic tank because the bathroom overflowed? Were you there when she needed to order more firewood for the winter 'cause she was freezing? Were you there to load the wood in the yard?"

"What do you want me to do? I was in school, man. It's not like I wasn't here because I didn't want to be. I was here at every break, at every chance, for the last four years. I was doing my best. I was here...."

"Yeah well, now that you're done with school, you gonna come back?"

"Well, I have to set up...."

"Exactly. You won't be here. I'll be here. I'm the one who took care of the family. I'm the one who will. I'm the one they call when they need someone. Were you there when we had the robbery in the house?"

"What robbery?"

"See, Shithead? Mom didn't even tell you, huh? You don't know half the shit you think you know. I'm the one who took care of them. Not you. I was here every day for them."

"You're right. I don't know. Do you want me to quit everything and come here for good?"

"Shut up. Shut the fuck up. Benny, hurry the fuck along! This asshole is going to jail for kidnapping! Just shut the fuck up! Stop talking to me. I don't ever want to talk to you again. You did this to me. You're the one who did this to me."

"I didn't do this to you. It's not my fault," said Steve. He waited a little bit, thought about how Charlie might take what he was going to say next. His frustration got the better of his compassion.

"Do you want me to be a screw-up like you so you can feel better? Is that what you want? Do you want me to fuck up my life as well? You think our family is better off with two fuckups than just one?"

Right away, he regretted saying it. Worse, his words did nothing to alleviate his frustration.

"Don't you know that our mother is not doing well?" asked Steve.

"Fuck you."

"Have you seen her lately? She wants to see you. Charlie, she's not going to make it if she falls this time. She's blaming herself for everything."

"I don't give a shit. Shut the fuck up!"

"I know you give a shit. Everyone else is still bugging the shit out of her. Aunt, uncles, Dad, you name it. They don't fuckin' leave her alone. You remember how some of them tried to beat her up and we couldn't stop them? I hated that. You hated that. You probably hated that more than me."

Steve sensed that his words were coming out with lots of bluster too. He wondered for a brief moment what his hypocrisy was.

He continued. "How can you tell me that it was all my fault? I didn't try hard to succeed so that I could get you. I just didn't have a choice."

"Will you shut the fuck up? I don't want to talk to you," said Charlie.

Charlie's voice had considerably weakened. Steve knew Charlie was listening.

"Mom needs us," said Steve, barely controlling his emotions that came from his own words. "She's sick, man, really sick."

"Don't fuckin' lecture me. Shut the fuck up."

"No, you shut up! You shut the fuck up!" Steve shouted at the top of his lungs. "I'm not playing games anymore! And neither are you! But you left me with no choice!"

Charlie didn't talk anymore. He leaned back and hid his face in the shadow of the interior light.

Steve toned his voice down.

"I'm sorry if I made you feel bad. I'm sorry I wasn't here for the family. I did my best to be here whenever I could. And I will never forget where I come from. If you fall, then she will fall. If she falls, then I fall. I'll tell you one thing, man, that's not gonna happen. I'm not gonna stop, Charlie. I'm just not...."

Steve fought hard to keep the twinge in his nose in check. He rolled his neck and wiped his face with his hand. Realizing he might possibly have smeared some blood that trickled from his nose, he wiped more thoroughly. He then checked for and found traces of blood on his hand, which he wiped on his pants. He continued to do what he could to buy time to keep his tears in check.

Charlie sighed and continued to hide his face in the darkness.

"Shit," he murmured.

CHAPTER SEVENTEEN
the fortuneteller

The previous winter, Charlie brought home his new girlfriend, Carmen. She was tall and beautiful with curves in all the right places. She wore a three-quarter length white mink coat and a one-piece satin dress that accentuated her broad shoulders, thin waist, and long legs. Her blond hair feathered beautifully over her shoulders, tapering at her hips, blending well with her cream-colored wardrobe. She was the kind of woman who could take the breath away from any guy. She moved like she knew what she looked like, with her nose held high and her back arched, accentuating her perky breasts.

As usual, Jasmine offered snacks and drinks and did her best to make Carmen feel comfortable. But once her gestures of good hospitality were completed, she left the room and didn't come out until Carmen and Charlie had left. Steve didn't like Carmen either. There was something about her bleached hair, her loud gum chewing and her fake fur coat that didn't fit the occasion. She looked too glitzy for meeting her boyfriend's family for the first time.

Charlie was oblivious to their disapproval of Carmen. In fact, he seemed proud to display his trophy. In between Carmen's frequent trips to the bathroom to "freshen up her face," he didn't even mind sharing with Steve how they had met or how their "make out" sessions went. Charlie and Steve rarely talked about these things with each other before.

"Man, Steve, that chick's a sex fiend."

"Really?"

"The weekend I met her, we went up to the Cascade Mountains and she fuckin' dry fucked me all night. She rode me for six hours straight."

"What's a dry fuck?"

"That's when she grinds your dick with your clothes still on."

Steve wondered why they hadn't just taken their clothes off and done it.

"That's called dry fucking?"

"Yeah, shit, I must've had blue balls for a whole week."

"What are blue balls?"

"You mean you don't know what blue balls are?"

Charlie made a face. It must be something painful, Steve guessed.

"No."

"That's when your dick's been hard for a long time without coming. Believe me, bro. You don't want it. It hurts like Hell."

"Oh. Why does it hurt?"

"I can't believe you never had it. Because, think about it. You get built up and built up without letting out. I mean, the pressure's got to go somewhere. Right? It's a pretty shitty thing to feel. It gets so numb, you feel like your dick's about to fall off."

"Dang. She rode you like that for hours?"

"Six. She's a fuckin' nympho. Little Often Annie."

Charlie seemed almost hypnotized by Carmen. She was the perfect ornament to decorate his new Corvette. Steve wished, as did Jasmine, that Charlie would use some of his eagerness to spend more time with the family. But then, if there was anyone who could understand why Charlie wanted to stay out with Carmen, it was Steve. After all, if she could dry fuck him for six hours straight and make his dick feel like it was going to fall off, imagine what she could do during the real thing.

Then, after several months of dating, Carmen accused Charlie of cheating. They had a fight on the beach and Charlie ended up getting arrested. He stood no chance against the beautiful, curvy, blond girl crying hysterically in the arms of a sympathetic policeman. He was handcuffed and thrown in jail faster than he could spell P-H-Y-S-I-C-A-L A-S-S-A-U-L-T. He had no chance in court, either. To the eyes of the white judge, the skinny, greasy, Asian boy who never looked anyone in the eye was as guilty as a dog. Whether Charlie had actually assaulted Carmen wasn't even the question; the fact that he had slept with a white girl was sin enough.

Charlie didn't hit Carmen nor did he cheat on her. That wasn't Charlie. He was busy trying to figure out why she did what she did when she hit herself. Nevertheless, feeling the odds against him and having no patience for arduous court procedures, Charlie settled out of court, forking over a huge amount of money. He had no money left. Charlie got dry fucked by Carmen again, only this time his dick wasn't the only thing falling off.

As soon as Steve heard of Charlie's mishap, he thought about the conversation he had with Jasmine a year before Carmen entered Charlie's life. The conversation took place while Steve was picking up Jasmine and Jang from the airport in Boston. Jasmine and Jang were returning from their first trip back to Korea since coming to America. Charlie had bought their airfare and Jasmine and Jang decided to make the most of his generosity. Although Jasmine seemed tired from the trip, she was excited to share her stories and the mountain of stuff she brought from the old country.

She managed to pack all the items in four large duffel bags, the maximum number for two people traveling internationally. On top of that, her carry-on bag was heavy enough to test Steve's strength. It was easy for Steve to spot her bags at the baggage claim area: all he had to do was look for the bags that were about to explode. Some of the wheels under the bags had collapsed from the weight. They spent hours just getting her bags out of the airport and strap them on to the vehicle. When she finally unpacked her bags, their living room was covered in clothing, furniture, exotic medicines, utensils, dishes, cups, ornaments, pictures, blankets, more clothing, and still more clothing. Even more amazing was how she remembered everything she brought, right down to the number of tiny bright-red briefs for Charlie and him.

The ride from the airport took about an hour, enough for a good conversation. They lived in the city of Rudbury, about forty miles north of Boston, on the New Hampshire border. Steve was happy to see Jasmine again and eager to hear about the trip. With the wind blowing inside the vehicle, Jasmine told him about her stepfamily in Korea, how the country changed, how the people changed, and how some things never changed. Jang drifted to sleep after ranting about how embarrassing it was for him to deal with the amount of stuff she insisted on bringing back.

"We basically went there to shop," he said, "from morning to night, all your mother wanted to do was to go out and get more stuff. I kept telling her to keep things light and do something fun for our vacation. Christ, all our relatives were busy trying to help her pack and load and unload the stuff all day long. It was full-time work for them. I was so embarrassed. I just went places by myself. I could never take her anywhere. Next time, I'll go back by myself."

"Well, go, then, go," said Jasmine, "I never told you not to go. Where would you go? Where would you stay? All your relatives and friends wanted from you was a handout. At least you got some room and board with mine."

"Yeah, well, I could've gone to many places. I was just worried about you."

"Nice try. No, you were broke after losing your money playing Hwatu (a Korean card game)."

"It's not fair that you keep all the money in the house to yourself. You have to at least give me my half."

"I did and you lost it all. You can't keep your money because you lose it all in Hwatu. You've been playing that game all your life and all you do is lose. At least try to win sometimes. Even I could do better with that much experience."

"I didn't play Hwatu. You didn't give me enough to play. My friends don't play that small. They'd probably have laughed at me. Where's the respect?"

"You can never get respect the way you live your life."

"Yeah, whatever. You are right and I'm always wrong. You guys can do whatever you want 'cause I don't care."

Whenever Jang finished the sentence with "You guys can do whatever you want 'cause I don't care," it meant he had run out of things to say. Indirectly, he was admitting his defeat.

Remarkably, by selling a lot of the items she brought to the Korean community, Jasmine not only ended up recovering much of the money they spent on the trip, but even making a tidy profit. Of course, the medicines she brought were the only ones Jang asked for in his time of need. She bought nothing for herself, not even a single piece of clothing.

One of her stories from the trip was about her session with a famous fortuneteller. Like most of the hardened villagers from the old country, Jasmine was a firm believer in the power of the unknown. She wanted to know about Charlie's future. According to a Korean legend, there are three ways of predicting one's fortune other than palm readings. One is to analyze the structure of a person's face. For example, a nose that curves down at the end indicates poverty, because money would glide away from the person. On the other hand, a nose with an enlarged tip is called a money nose because money can be collected there. Their measurements and explanations are precise, almost scientific, down to the millimeter. Steve neither accepted nor rejected this method. A person's future could indeed be predicted by studying the expressions on his or her face. But, the external and internal pressures of society can help shape a person's face. So which comes first? Steve also bet that these ancient philosophers had never seen races other than their own. How would they explain a white man's nose, which is larger than the average-size Asian nose? Or dark skin? To Steve, the method wasn't valid unless it worked on all races.

The second way of predicting someone's fortune involved analyzing an individual's name and birthday. By figuring out how the name was created and how the celestial bodies aligned during the birth, a fortuneteller could make an "educated" guess about the fate of the individual.

Steve was also impartial to this school of thought. As much as he respected the ancient philosophers, the idea that a person's fate could rest on the creation of his/her name and what celestial bodies were present at the time of his/her birth seemed too far-fetched to be taken seriously.

These two methods were generally considered scholarly in Korea, and the fortunetellers using these methods were highly respected. Many of them devoted their lives to proving the predictive power of these approaches. Their offices were filled with books, and they served their clients like teachers meeting students. It was a tradition that most people in Korea visited them before getting married, making career moves, or finding appropriate names for their newborns.

The third way was the most controversial and least respected. A fortuneteller would call on a spirit from the other side, usually one they had already bonded with, to enter into his/her body. Once the spirit settled into the fortuneteller, the powers of the supernatural world would allow the fortuneteller to predict the future. These fortunetellers would only accept certain clients. Despite many phonies, some of these readings had been documented to be miraculously accurate. Steve didn't like Jasmine visiting this kind of fortuneteller because he didn't want her exposed to the power of the unknown world. Legend had it that once the door swung open for an individual, it would forever be a two-way door for that person. Steve figured everything had a price, and to the spirits, it wouldn't be money.

Upon the strong recommendation of her mother, Jasmine visited this kind of fortuneteller, one with an especially prominent reputation for her amazing predictions. The fortuneteller was so popular that she didn't accept new clients. Even during a session, her phone wouldn't stop ringing. The fortuneteller answered all the calls herself, booking only certain callers who gave her the correct vibes. Sometimes, the fortuneteller swore at the callers and angrily hung up the phone for no reason.

"Oh, not you. Anyone but you. You are bad! May you rot in Hell!" she would say.

The fortuneteller readily accepted Jasmine. In fact, the fortuneteller even cast aside some of her other appointments to make room for her. This wasn't atypical for Jasmine. For some reason, most fortunetellers loved to read for her, sometimes volunteering. Maybe it was because she was the perfect sucker, or maybe it was because her pain was so visible to them. This fortuneteller hadn't even accepted any money from Jasmine.

When Jasmine first saw the famous fortuneteller, she thought that the old lady was illiterate. The fortuneteller struggled to write Charlie's name. When the spirit entered her body, however, she wrote more clearly and also spoke much more eloquently. To Jasmine's amazement, the fortuneteller even wrote some of her stuff in English. It was as if Jasmine was looking at a different person! She was scared and wanted to get out of the room, but her overwhelming desire to know the fate of her vulnerable son outweighed all of that.

Looking straight into Jasmine's eyes, the fortuneteller's first words were, "Ah, it's you. You've come back to me from America. I'm glad to see you again." Tears welled up in the fortuneteller's eyes. Without any reason, Jasmine began to cry. The old lady's voice transported her back to her childhood, to the time when she saw her father die in front of her. They sat there in silence for much of the night, crying. Jasmine never felt so secure in her entire life, like a little girl being embraced by her father.

The fortuneteller told Jasmine that Charlie would soon meet a yellow-haired woman who would take everything Charlie owned. This woman would be very bad for him. She accurately predicted that Charlie was an individual who could succeed at anything, but had even more potential to fail. She warned that Charlie was on the verge of acquiring a sickness that had been handed down from his forefathers. If not contained, Charlie would die. But she also said that Charlie still had a chance to change; that only Jasmine's love could prevent the disease from spreading.

As any skeptic would, Steve decided to play devil's advocate. He mentioned to Jasmine that sometimes events actually come true simply because people anticipate that they will. Also, the vagueness of the words used by these fortunetellers could be interpreted in too many ways to be considered accurate. It is easy to make people believe in something they already believe in or in something they want to believe in. Still, if Jasmine had described it correctly, Steve was impressed with the fortuneteller's predictions. Unlike others, she was detailed. Steve couldn't find any other way to interpret her words. And, a year later, they had indeed proven true with Charlie, right down to the time, date, age, and form of settlement with Carmen.

At Jasmine's request, the fortuneteller also predicted Steve's fate. She predicted that he would be in a job where many people would respect him. He would be involved in a life of scholarly occupation, sitting behind a desk all the time, like some kind of a writer. He would have a prosperous life. He would be a good husband and a good father. He would end up taking care of Jasmine and Jang in their winter years.

Steve chuckled inside when he heard about him being a deskman. The fortuneteller was definitely wrong about that. Even before his graduation, though he hadn't told anyone, Steve wanted to be a martial arts teacher more than anything else. He had already started a small club in college that had become fairly successful. In fact, he was able to earn enough income to cover some of his living expenses. After graduation, he wanted to abandon his education as an engineer and start a full-time business teaching martial arts. People would be respecting him in a different way, and certainly not because of his scholarly attributes. In fact, what he wanted to do was far from scholarly, maybe even the opposite. Imagine that: Steve, a writer.

CHAPTER EIGHTEEN
the boy scout

They arrived at the Catherlina police station and parked their vehicles on the street. Although the building had a well-manicured lawn, it seemed too small to be a police station. No policemen or police cars were visible. Steve wondered if they had any cells there at all. Benny and Steve got out of the vehicle. Jang, who had parked behind them, also got out. No one seemed to be in any hurry to go anywhere. Steve took a big breath of the night air, thinking it might be his last taste of freedom for a couple of days.

He thought about how he should approach his problem with the police. How does one say:

"Please lock up my brother, he is on drugs. And, oh yeah, if possible, lock me up too, so that I can watch over him. But only for a short while, just a day or so, until I can come up with a plan."

As crazy as it sounded, Steve felt confident that the police would understand him. They must have dealt with this kind of problem before. The beach was a mecca for drug problems. The police would probably welcome the plea of someone who was trying to do *their* job.

Steve turned around and peeked inside the vehicle. Charlie was still sitting there.

"We're here," said Steve, matter-of-factly.

Charlie didn't move. Steve could sense another confrontation coming, not that it would even matter to Steve if Charlie threw another big fit. With the police station so close, it would only speed up their plan, which was fine for him. He was ready.

Steve leaned on the vehicle and crossed his arms, and decided to wait. It was Charlie's turn to make the next move.

"Hey, what's the hold up?" asked Jang, who had done a fine job of staying by his vehicle, but was now walking hastily towards them.

Steve quickly shook his head at Jang. Jang took the hint and backed off. He walked back to his vehicle and fumbled in his left chest pocket for another cigarette.

Benny walked in front of the vehicle with his arms crossed and leaned on the bumper. Steve continued to lean on the side of the vehicle with his arms also crossed. It was getting chilly. He noticed the cuts and bruises on his forearms. One of the buttons on his golf shirt was missing. His pants were covered in dirt, traces of blood, and debris from the ditch. He didn't want to move, however.

Everyone was still.

A middle-aged woman passed by holding a poodle with a red ribbon around its neck. The little poodle tried to sniff Steve and the gang intensely in the little time it had before being dragged away. When it got to Steve, the poodle took a whiff of his pants and looked at Steve curiously, as if it detected something abnormal. The woman whisked her dog away and checked the scene: Jang was chain-smoking by the next vehicle over, Benny was staring blankly out into the street, and Steve was absolutely still. No one said a word, no one acknowledged the poodle. The woman scurried away quickly with the poodle, seeming to be offended. Watching the poodle being yanked away by the chain around its neck didn't lift Steve's spirits. He would feel it himself soon enough.

Steve leaned inside the vehicle to check up on Charlie.

"Hey, we're here, man," said Steve. "What's up?"

Charlie remained silent.

Steve waited a moment. "Shit, what's up?" he asked again.

"I don't want to go. You idiot!" said Charlie. Somehow Steve felt like Charlie was talking to him normally for the first time today.

"You wanted to come here. You said to come here."

"I'm not going in, Stupid. God!" Charlie let out another huge sigh.

Charlie was frustrated that Steve hadn't recognized his bluff.

He thought for sure that everyone hated the police. All his friends did. All the cops were good for was to give him and his friends parking or driving tickets, break up parties, bust them for drugs, and harass them for no reason. Charlie knew these cops, these losers, didn't really have respect for the law; they only enjoyed the hunt. These assholes drove more recklessly, drank more heavily, and snorted more cocaine than all of his friends combined. They were the real criminals. At least Charlie and his friends knew what they were. These assholes didn't. The worst criminals were the ones who didn't know that they were bad. Charlie truly hated these guys. His friends hated these guys. If there was ever a common enemy among all his friends, it was these so-called cops. Charlie couldn't begin to count how many hours he and his friends had spent ranting about these losers. Just because they had badges they thought they had the courage. Real courage was knowing who you were, good or bad, especially if you were bad. These assholes thought they were sent from Heaven to snort cocaine and drive drunk. They actually thought they were above the law. If not for their stupid badges, Charlie and his friends would've done some serious butt whipping on them. The cops were nothing without badges. Just once he wished he could tell them to put down their guns and badges and arrest him like a man, hand-to-hand, mano-y-mano. He would've had a field day fucking them up, crushing their soft donut-filled guts with his back kick, flattening their snorting noses with a spinning heel kick, breaking their never-ending-blabbering jaws – *You have the right to remain silent. You have the right to...* – with a right cross and take out all their teeth. See if they could recite the Miranda rights without their fuckin' teeth. God! He hated them.

But Charlie now realized the cops represented something totally different to Steve. He had to sigh, not out of frustration for Steve's naiveté, but because of his own stupidity in the bluff. Charlie should've known better. Steve was too naive, too straight, to take the bluff. He still considered the police to be a friend. A friend! Steve was forever the boy scout, the last boy scout Charlie would ever know. Steve had never been nor ever known any other way but straight. He was a dreamer, and amazingly enough, even after all these years, the dirt of the real world has never tainted his boyish ideals. As much as Charlie hated this naive quality in Steve, he also admired him for having the courage to believe.

Steve wasn't stupid. Charlie knew that. Without Steve, Charlie knew that the family would've suffered more. Steve supplied the stability for the family. Everyone took comfort in his ability to handle problems. Steve was always where he was supposed to be, where he was expected to be. And now Charlie could see his little brother all grown up. Everything he conjured up about Steve in his head – the predictable, overachieving, overbearing, goody two-shoes – wasn't someone he hated, but rather, admired. And deep in his heart, Charlie had known it all along.

Charlie realized why Steve was here now. His little brother wanted to bring him home because he loved him. *Because he loved him.*

"I'll go home," said Charlie.

Jubilation filled Steve's body from the magic of the words that came out of Charlie's mouth. Something imploded in his heart and filled his body with uncontrollable joy. His eardrums popped. His knees shook and he had to restrain himself from screaming and leaping. He felt his hair stand straight up and he could hardly catch his breath. *I'll go home.* No words ever sounded sweeter. *I'll go home.* The words kept echoing in his brain, his now hollow brain, because all thoughts flew out of his head with the implosion. The fact that he couldn't show his happiness only prolonged the agony of joy.

"What?" asked Steve.

Steve wanted to make it sound like he was agitated. He needed to contain his feelings and downplay the whole situation. He certainly didn't want Charlie to think that he was gloating from winning the battle. Still, Steve couldn't contain himself and worried that he might not have concealed his elation. Charlie could change his mind; he always did. But right now Charlie seemed sure, as if that was what he intended to do all along, that he never had any desire to go to the police in the first place.

How could I have missed that? Steve wondered.

"I'd rather go home than stay here. They know me here. I don't like these Assholes. They're Dicks," said Charlie.

"Whoa, man. Make up your mind," said Steve.

Steve dared to push Charlie a little further. This time, the effects of persuasion were on his side. The more he pushed, the more Charlie settled into his decision.

"I told you. I wanna go home. I'm fuckin' tired. Benny, get in the car and drive."

Charlie was now in charge as well, leading the way home himself. Steve couldn't be happier to yield his position, like a good little brother should. Benny turned around, bewildered. He looked at Steve. Steve shrugged his shoulders in response. Benny tilted his head and smiled a little. The gesture caused a second implosion of joy in Steve because he was sure now that he wasn't hallucinating.

"Fine," said Steve, still trying to sound irritated. With that, he stamped the official seal of approval by looking at Jang, who was lighting up another cigarette while leaning on the side of his vehicle. He yelled out, "Hey Dad, Charlie wants to go home. You just follow us from behind like before, okay?"

"What?" asked Jang, obviously surprised. He almost dropped his precious piece from his mouth, but caught it just in time. Charlie must've gotten his reflexes from Jang, thought Steve.

"Just follow us home," Steve was happy to repeat.

"What are you talking about? Why are we going home? We should lock that rotten boy in jail for good!"

There was no malice in Jang's voice. Steve could tell Jang was happy about the unexpected turn of events, too.

"Please cut it out," said Steve.

Steve didn't want Jang to provoke another outburst from

Charlie. If anyone could still rev Charlie up, it was the older version of Charlie himself.

"Oh, whatever. Do whatever you want 'cause I don't care anymore," said Jang.

"Well, let's go home, Benny," said Steve.

Steve was careful not to carry on a longer conversation than that with Benny. Benny was Charlie's friend, and Steve had to show Charlie that he wasn't here to impose on anything of Charlie's.

"Okay, mang," said Benny, catching Steve's subtle melodic voice, quickly getting into the vehicle, and shutting the door with an exclamation point. He didn't even buckle his seat belt.

"Mang" sounded so good. *We're going home!*

CHAPTER NINETEEN
the cold wind

As they cut along the dark highway, the group was in a trance. Steve had made Benny leave the interior light on during the ride to the police station, but now he had him turn it off. The darkness brought out the throbbing in his face. The adrenaline had left his body without him realizing it and had taken the rest of his energy with it. He leaned his face against the window, hoping to get some coldness on his face. It helped a little, but the strain brought more aches. The most difficult ache was the emotional drain. He had nothing left.

Soon the rattling of the ride rocked him to sleep. He fought hard to stay awake, but the quarter flash of streaming trees, overpass bridges, signs, and streetlights hypnotized him further into dreamland. If he had known it was going to take this much effort to bring Charlie home, he never would've done it. It took all his energy and all his spirit to lead him to this point. He was aware that he had to stay alert until the end, but he was done. The fat lady had sung. He didn't have any energy left to withstand another one of Charlie's mood swings.

Luckily, Charlie seemed more exhausted than Steve, snoring loudly from his crunched-up position. Even in his most benign condition, Charlie still appeared desperate. Who knew how many sleepless nights he had trying to right his wrongs. All Charlie really wanted was respect – to make everyone around him proud of him. Charlie's first mistake was his attempt to hang respect on the walls of his living room.

They finally got off highway I-782 South and onto the connecting local route 12, Leslo Drive. The Lee family lived on this street, three miles down from the winding road. Just about every drive from the house required this road. Steve had driven this road so many times that he had memorized every twist and turn.

Sometimes, during his drives back from college, Steve would entertain himself by pretending that the road had come alive for him – like a worm squirming to straighten itself out before him. The faster he drove, the more it straightened. Then he would imagine that the world was moving around him, as if he mattered that much, as if he was the center of the universe. The houses, the trees, the shiny crest of the earth, all welcoming him home. The world was his. Occasionally, vehicles from the opposite direction forced him back to reality, reminding him that the world was too large to care who he was, that he was nothing more than one of billions of human beings, one of millions of species on the planet, one of millions of specks in the galaxy, one of millions of galaxies in the universe – but nevertheless he would dream again.

Did it really matter to know what mattered and what didn't?

Not according to Vincent Nagallo.

"Everything is relative, Steve," echoed the words of his best friend in high school.

"What do you mean, 'relative'?"

"I mean that nothing is permanent in the universe. Every fact, every viewpoint, everything, is only relative to the point of its origin. And your origin is different than mine. So nothing is absolutely real."

As usual, Steve decided to challenge Vincent. But he knew Vincent would come up with a rebuttal that would probably dwarf his challenge. Vincent was smart.

"What about one plus one? It will always equal two. That's for sure. Are you telling me that's not a fact?"

"Well, yeah, it is. One plus one is two, but your 'one' could be different than my 'one'. The theory of relativity states that objects of time and space change with different origins. For example, in the case of time, if you travel at the speed of light, your one-second is quite different than my one second. Yours is longer, much longer, because the speed of light contracts time and space. In that sense, your one plus one does not necessarily equal two for me.

In fact, yours will equal roughly two years of mine."

"It's only a theory, Vincent, Einstein could be wrong."

"Perhaps. And that's exactly the point I am getting at. We should never believe anything absolutely. We must keep our minds open and understand that everything in life is relative. Views and ideas can always be changed. Everything can be changed. What we perceive as big might be small for others, what we perceive as bad might be perceived by others as good."

"I know that. But there are certain things we agree on that are absolutely true."

"Like what?" asked Vincent.

"Well like...Hitler. You can't possible think that Hitler was good? Hitler was the enemy of the world."

"Ah, but you are wrong."

"What do you mean 'wrong'? You mean he was good? After killing millions of innocent lives? Gimme a break!"

"No, I'm not saying he was good. To me, he was evil, a monster. But I'm also aware that is only my opinion, that he wasn't absolute evil. If he had won World War II, I'm sure people would've viewed him quite differently. They would probably view Churchill and Roosevelt as bad. Also, all the histories of the world were written by people with their own visions. Their relative visions. No one should believe absolutely that everything happened exactly the way it was written. Everything is relative, Steve. Nothing in life is ever definite. We mustn't ever forget that. This knowledge is what separates us from the rest of society. It makes us free."

Steve was frustrated, even desperate. Not because he wanted to win the debate, but because he felt there had to be something absolute in people's lives that Vincent couldn't deny. Otherwise what's the point? There had to be something that was so powerful, so obvious that Vincent had to agree to it unconditionally. Steve had to let Vincent know.

Vincent and Steve had lots of conversations like this during their high school years. Debating with Vincent was always tough for Steve. Vincent graduated at the top of their class, easily. He had answers to everything and had proofs and theorems to back him up. He was always one step ahead of Steve. Throughout high school, Steve and Vincent supported each other academically. Steve supported Vincent in math and Vincent supported him in everything else. Vincent was Steve's biggest cheerleader in sports and his best teacher in academics. They hung out together so much that the kids in school thought they were elitist snobs. While most of the other boys went out with girls on Friday nights, Vincent and Steve discussed politics, philosophy, religion, and science at their homes.

"That's so dire. Why do we bother living then? If nothing is real, why do we have to struggle so much? We should all just die."

"Who knows, Steve, we might already be dead and the dead might be living. You can't really say we are living. How can we be sure until we are dead? You can't make a clear judgment without seeing both ways. Many philosophers have pondered this question for centuries. Some believe that we only live in the dreams of other people, and that when they wake up then you are dead."

"Well, the fact that I can question my living must mean that I live now. Otherwise, why would I question my life? If I can question it, doesn't that mean that I'm liberated enough from conventional thinking to make a clear judgment?"

"Yeah, but a moment ago, you didn't question it. Were you dead then, and this sudden awareness made you alive? If so, then how do you know you aren't dead again to some other awareness you haven't come across? Think about dreams that seem so real until you wake up. We could be dreaming now and we wouldn't even know it."

"Shit, Vincent, all this seems so bogus. I know there is something permanent in our lives. I just know it. Maybe you and I haven't been exposed to it yet. Maybe this is something that comes with time."

The conversation seemed so blatantly wrong that Steve was

sure that one correct comment from him would earn him a victory. There seemed to be so many easy answers, yet he couldn't think of any. It seemed ridiculous to him that nothing in life was permanent, but somehow Vincent proved it. Numbers, time and space, good and evil, beginning and end, everything Steve ever believed in was forced to disappear.

Steve often thought about those debates since then, and continued his search for the one thing that was absolute that Vincent couldn't deny. He thought about it so much that it became a habit. He wanted desperately to believe that life was special, that there was a greater meaning out there. But as he grew older, he was able to see more of Vincent's view than his own. Changes were everywhere and rapid. People aged, friends changed, homes moved, money passed, thoughts forgotten, and time kept ticking away – reminding him that nothing stayed the same; that nothing really mattered. He was discouraged and felt jaded. He searched and searched, but to no avail. Is there anything that mattered eternally?

Then one day it happened.

It was delivered to him. On a clear night, feeling alone and hungry as he walked down the high slope of the campus after being cooped up in a library for the day studying for a college exam, he was forced to ponder the same question. What is constant in this world? There was indeed nothing in life that was permanent. He could die right here, he thought, and his death wouldn't make any difference to this world, other than the brief sympathies of the still living. He was tired of believing. What was the point of living? The point of struggle? All it offered was pain. God gave him a heart to feel pain, but not enough of a brain to understand why. Then, just as he closed his eyes to summon up his energy to forget once again, a sweeping wind whisked away every part of him, and delivered him a message, the answer. He ran home that night; he thought it was pain.

But soon he felt it. It was an answer that enlightened not his mind, but his heart. It was clear and gradually it changed his life.

The answer was there all along, watching him, protecting him, waiting for him, until he was ready for it. Steve learned that the pain he felt that night wasn't pain at all. It was joy, the joy of discovery. Later he shared his message with others. Some years later, he even wrote a letter to the messenger, thanking it. It was no accident that he met the messenger, the cold wind. Nothing in life, he realized, was a coincidence.

Dear Cold Wind,

I was barely a child when you first came to me. As I eagerly watched the sunset and hoped my marble game would never end, you reminded me that it was time to go home. I didn't know time then, but I knew the sunset was my curfew because of the chilliness you brought afterwards. As the crisp fall leaves scratched the surface of the street before being lifted off the air, you came to me for the first time and urged me to go home. Your cold-hearted reminder slowly swept away my innocence. I didn't understand why good things had to end. Why couldn't they last forever? I was having so much fun.

As the sun slowly came down, your reminder turned into a command. You screeched and pushed me. My hair blew wildly and my eyes could barely open from your impatient persuasion. I wished you would go away. I didn't think much of you afterwards. I thought you were just a passing stranger.

From then on, you came to me every fall. I

tried to face you each time, but one sweep of your magnificent presence would numb my heart and leave me helpless. Each meeting hurt me like the first time. I didn't know who you were, and that was the worst pain of all.

Then one night, you finally revealed yourself to me. As each year before, your scent and presence reminded me of our first encounter. Unlike myself, however, you remained the same. You always have. In fact, you were the only one that hadn't changed, and, I realized, you never will. For a moment I wished I could be you. No, even more, a being powerful enough to stop you. Yet you passed through me as if I wasn't there, that I didn't matter. You didn't even bother to laugh at my momentary silly hope. You were your cruelest that day as you failed to sweep me away with you.

My life has turned for the better since then. Now there is only spring breeze in my life. At times, another cold wind reminds me so much of you, and I wonder where you are, where I am. I can feel you more as each day goes by. I know you'll be back for me someday. Oh, how bittersweet would that be.

The answer was there all along. It was everywhere. If we open our hearts, if we learn to accept ourselves, then we can truly feel how special we are, how beautiful we are. We have the power to touch Heaven. That is why we are left here: to feel it, to discover it, to appreciate it. Life is precious because it's not permanent. Life is beautiful because it's not permanent. The absolute truth in life is love. The love that is in all of us. If we accept the changes, the changes in our lives, then we can truly feel the power of love; if we can't, then love only feels like pain. Love cannot be relative because nothing else can compare to it. Not even the vast universe. Love is ever lasting because we don't last.

Vincent was wrong.

CHAPTER TWENTY
coming home, part I

Charlie woke up and began fidgeting as they neared the house, but Steve was too occupied with his own thoughts to notice him. All Steve could think about was taking a long, hot shower, eating a warm meal, and going to bed. He was ready to sleep – hard! – with his body glued to the sheets. He would deal with tomorrow, tomorrow. Just for tonight, Steve wanted everything to be normal, like the old days: with Mom and Dad and Brother and Sister in one big happy home, passing bowls of rice, drinking hot cups of tea, watching TV, even if he had to pretend.

Jasmine would be elated to see Charlie. At the first sight of him, she would take a deep sigh of relief and allow her bad dream to dissipate. Then she would go to work on Charlie. In her own way, she would convince Charlie to stay long after tonight. Charlie had no chance. He wouldn't even know what hit him, she was that good. All she needed was a chance to work her magic spell.

First, she wouldn't speak to Charlie, except to offer him food and nourishment. She wouldn't even say hello. She knew that Charlie didn't like formalities. Jasmine would let him know in other ways how happy she was to see him. Charlie would have a warm meal and hot tea by his side as he relaxed in the living room. She wouldn't even stay with him. She would only reappear to bring him more snacks to munch on or another hot cup of roasted barley tea. She would communicate through her actions: how she prepared his meal, how she timed her entrances, how she made everything so easy for him.

Charlie might not realize the amount of detail that went into making him feel so comfortable, but he would undoubtedly feel it, little by little, creeping into his heart. He would find the meal exactly the way he wanted it – freshly-made rice, spicy Kimchi to tease his soul, marinated cod to quench his ocean obsession, and the dry, roasted, salted seaweed wrap to go with the hot barley tea – something he longed for. And when he dozed off watching TV after a satisfying meal, there would be the perfect pillow waiting next to him. He would drift in and out of sleep, as he usually did with the TV on, and there would be his cozy comforter, covering him, just enough to warm him but not enough to suffocate him. The TV would be on. Charlie would avoid silence.

Later, when Charlie would be in a deeper sleep, Jasmine would bring another blanket to cover him and finally turn the TV off, as she had done so many times before. She would stay awake just to do so. Then, finally, she would watch her son for the first time, looking at his face, seeing her baby, noticing the increasing wrinkles, how much weight he had lost, how much he had suffered. She would cry, lamenting how her baby had suffered because of her.

Deep in his dream, Charlie would hear her. Jasmine's tears would slip under his skin and into his bloodstream, creating energy. It would multiply a billion fold, rising to a prodigious volume and sweeping through his body. It would be like a giant avalanche, rumbling down every corner of his body, crushing all his mistakes, all his pain, all his guilt, and leaving him in a pure white winter wonderland.

When he awoke to the bright morning, Jasmine would bring him yet another fresh cup of hot roasted barley tea, but this time with some corn flavor in it, creating a heavenly aroma. His breakfast would already be prepared, with all his favorite dishes elaborately laid out in a simple and informal way. How she prepared them without making a single noise in the kitchen located next to the living room where he slept, Charlie would never know. Charlie would eat again, feeling secure, feeling loved. For the first time in a very long time, he would eat, not because he was hungry, but because he wanted to.

Charlie would realize what he had missed while he was away, and that he was missed. He had just felt the strongest force in the world: a mother's love for her child. He would exhale, knowing that he could always be a kid here, no matter how badly he messed up. He would realize how ignorant he was to take for granted the most precious thing he ever possessed. Love was precious – oh, he had learned that, especially during the last couple of months. He would stay. Even if he did leave his home again, he would come back. And all it would take was one look from Jasmine.

With a quick left turn into the driveway, they were home. The long driveway looked rather desolate at this time of the night. The light in the house was on, although the lot was dark and bugs were plentiful. Benny got out of the vehicle and stretched. Steve took a quick glance at Charlie and eagerly got out of the vehicle, too. The ground felt good to him. A couple of hours ago, he thought he would never feel this turf again. He stretched his arms out as wide as he could, trying to shake off the heaviness of the night. His face throbbed more and he wondered if he had any marks on him. He didn't want Jasmine to see them.

Jang came over. Steve noticed Charlie hadn't come out of the vehicle yet. When he looked inside, Charlie was still sitting in his seat. Jang stuck his head inside the vehicle, crowding Steve.

"Aren't you coming out?" asked Jang.

After pausing, Jang spoke again. "Hey, I'm talking to you. Aren't you coming out?"

"No, I don't want to."

"We are here. We are home. Come out," continued Jang. "What is it now? Something wrong again? What is it?"

"I don't want to go in, I told you." Jang's persuasion strengthened Charlie's new rebellion. "Everyone can go in. I'm going to Ashton with Benny."

Ashton was the town next to Rudbury, about ten miles away. The Lee family lived there before they moved here. The city had more than its share of drug problems. All of Charlie's friends were from there. Ashton was once known for its industrial strength from the mill factories, but now it struggled with high unemployment and an influx of immigrants. Bullets frequently flew in the city projects.

A pizza deliveryman was shot to death at point blank range while delivering a pizza. A woman was shot in the back while walking home from a grocery store by a bored teenager. But the worst story was about a hitchhiker who was picked up by an evil couple. They tortured the poor man for forty-eight hours straight, beating him, slicing his skin repeatedly with a razor and adding tenderizer to his open wounds, before killing him. Then there was that riot in Ashton some years back that had made the headlines of every newspaper in the country. A nationally syndicated magazine rated Ashton as one of the worst cities in the country to live in at the time.

Jang continued his assault on Charlie. The boss was back in town. Maybe being at home justified that position, especially when his wife was so close.

"What? What Ashton? What are you talking about?" asked Jang.

"Benny, get in the car and drive," ordered Charlie.

Benny looked at Steve. Steve shook his head.

"What's up, mang?" asked Benny.

"Let's go to Ashton," said Charlie.

"Christ, make up your mind!" yelled Jang. He was revving up.

"You see what you've gotten me into? See this shit? I hope you're happy, Shithead," said Charlie, looking at Steve.

Steve panicked. He was a shithead again. Certainly better than a motherfucker, but nonetheless, a shithead was a shithead. Steve stayed silent, though. He wanted to wait and see how things would turn out. He was too tired to do anything else. He hoped Jang would do the same. But, alas, Jang was only warming up.

Charlie and Jang fought constantly, especially as Charlie got older. They fought about anything and everything. All they had to do was say one thing to each other and it would trigger streams of shouting, mostly from Jang. Then Jang would find a way to get Jasmine involved. Eventually a whole new argument would erupt between them. It almost seemed like Jang wanted to blame Jasmine for everything.

Of course, if the arguments were about something very serious, like Charlie's college applications, then all Hell broke loose. When Charlie was about to embark on a new college life, the Lee family was thrilled. Charlie was the first of his generation to enter college. Each night Jang ended up screaming at Charlie about his mishandling of college applications, which college he should go to, and how he should prepare for his career. All Jang did was yell. He never actually helped Charlie with them. Charlie did his best to avoid Jang's moods, but he wasn't that patient himself. Eventually, the ongoing arguments would force Jasmine to join in, and the blame game would start between Jasmine and Jang. She would blame him for not taking action and he would blame her for taking too many actions. She would then refute that she did what she did because of what he didn't do. He would reply that he couldn't do what he was supposed to do because she already screwed everything up before he had a chance to do anything. The cycle continued over and over, like a hamster on a wheel, until both were sapped of their might. They would shout all night and Steve would have to stay on guard to prevent them from physically hurting each other.

The fights were mainly due to Jang's frustration, as he felt helpless about not being able to properly prepare his son for college. He was reminded of how he wasn't able to go to school like other people because of his misfortune. He had received only a ninth grade education but with straight A's. Jang wanted what was best for his son, but he also wanted some kind of payback for his own misfortune. If Jasmine blamed herself for everything, then Jang blamed everything but himself.

Each and every fight between Jang and Jasmine was difficult for Steve to bear. He hated seeing Jasmine leave for work the next day to put in another sixteen-hour shift. And when she came home, she would cook dinner and clean the house, without taking a break, while Jang would eat the meal she cooked and watch TV with his hands in his pockets. Then, just when she would finally find some time to relax, he would start the cycle all over again.

In truth, Jang cared too much about Charlie. He just didn't know how to handle Charlie's temperament, which was all too similar to his own. It scared him. He didn't want his sickness to spread to his son. And when Charlie rebelled, he interpreted it as the disease spreading and tried what he thought was the best way to stop it. It had an adverse effect on Charlie and reached a point where Charlie felt the home he loved became the home he hated.

"This is unbelievable! And I'm going crazy! What the Hell do you want from me?! You wanted to come here, so we're here. Why are you doing this to me?" asked Jang.

"Benny, let's go. Come on." Charlie pleaded with Benny. "I don't fucking want to be here a second longer. You know I hate this shit. Why the fuck aren't you helping me?"

Jang stuck his head further inside the vehicle, ready to holler. This time Steve intervened.

"Stop, Dad. Just stop!" yelled Steve, desperately.

Jang backed away a little, but Steve's intervention only reinforced Charlie's reasons for not wanting to come out of the vehicle.

"Come on Benny, for Christ's sake. What more do you have to see?" asked Charlie.

"Yo, mang. I don't want to go to Ashton. I'm kinda tired. I wanna go home."

"Just drive me there then. I gotta get my car back from the beach. Someone might take it. Just get me to Ashton. Get me the Hell out of this shit hole."

"I don't think you should do that, mang."

"I told you I gotta get my car back. It'll get stripped there in no time if I leave it there overnight. That fuckin' place is crowded with thieves."

That was Charlie. Still scheming.

"Yo, mang...."

"You guys can do whatever you want 'cause I don't care

anymore. I'm tired of this nonsense," said Jang as he headed towards the house. He stopped half way, however, and decided to wait there. He looked awkward as he stood still. There were no cigarettes left for him to smoke.

Good, Steve thought, now let's see if it's not too late to use the softer approach to coax Charlie out.

"Fuck it. You won't drive me there, I'll fuckin' walk."

Charlie got out of the vehicle. Steve took a few steps towards him and was met with a lightning fast punch to the left side of his jaw. Again, it was so fast he didn't even have time to flinch. Again, Steve was disappointed by his delayed response. What good were all those blocks he practiced if he couldn't even see the punches coming? But then, Charlie was always faster than he. Steve knew he could never be that fast. In any case, the punch didn't follow through all the way. It didn't hurt him. Charlie still had compassion left.

Steve spat out a large chunk of blood, wondering where Charlie had gotten the strength to punch. How could he still have any energy? Certainly, Steve didn't have anymore of it. The punch hurt him, not from its blow, but from the anticipation of what might come next and how helpless he was from preventing it. For the first time today, Steve felt defeated. He was now only a shell of himself. He let his guard down too early and his adrenaline had left him prematurely.

"Asshole! I didn't want to come here. Get away from me. Leave me alone." Charlie walked across the front lawn towards the street. Steve followed him, desperate to stop him, not knowing what else to do.

"You promised you'd come home. Keep your promise," said Steve, using the little brother voice to draw out his big brother's compassion.

"I did. I got here now, didn't I? Now I'm going home, my home, and you can't stop me. I did come here. Didn't I? I never said I'd go inside the house, did I?" asked Charlie.

He seemed to gain confidence from his own reasoning. He even offered a smile, more like a smirk, as if he had planned the whole thing. It was good, as it always was, to best his little brother.

"Benny, man, I don't want to walk. It's fuckin' far. Just give me a ride 'til Ashton. Will you?"

Charlie was charismatic, like a salesman going home after a long day of work. 'Just give me a ride 'til Ashton. Will you?' Something a friend would say to a friend. Charlie could be so devious. He could carry you to the top of a mountain or the bottom of the ocean if he wanted to, and he was feeling it now.

Steve stopped in his tracks. He turned to Benny, worried. This time, he wasn't sure if Benny could resist Charlie. Benny looked back at Steve. They both knew what the other was thinking – they had lost.

"No, no mang, I...I don't want to go there. I told you, I'm tired. I'm going home."

"Fuck you then. Fuck you all. I'm outta here. It's no big deal. Just maybe three miles down and I'll call my friends at the payphone and have them pick me up. That's it. You didn't think I could walk, did you?"

Charlie's silhouette faded in the darkness. Without looking back, he said, "Benny, man, I'll fuckin' deal with you later."

His navy blue sweatshirt blended into the night. With a quick right turn he disappeared over the corner bush.

What could Steve do? Charlie did come home as he promised. And Charlie was correct, he hadn't promised to go into the house. Steve wrestled with the thought of whether he should try to hold Charlie down again. He decided not to. There was no justification for that this time. Last time, it was to prevent Charlie from jumping in front of an oncoming vehicle, but this time it wouldn't be anything other than using brute force to drag Charlie inside. Like a criminal. That really would be kidnapping. If Steve treated Charlie like a criminal, Charlie might act like one.

What then? He thought about following Charlie again, but

what would that lead to when Charlie's friends picked him up? He couldn't barge into somebody else's vehicle, especially one owned by one of Charlie's hoodlum friends. He would get shot. Why hadn't he thought of that when he first chased Charlie before? Steve felt silly. Who was he trying to act like, God? As if he knew what was best for everybody. Charlie was right. Who the Hell did he think he was? Sometimes, people had to know their limitations. Steve did show Charlie how much he cared about him. He had endured hours of Charlie's emotional outbursts and had pushed Charlie to have a heart-to-heart talk with him. Steve had done what he had to do, what he could do. There was nothing more. He had done enough. Now he needed to come to his senses and worry about his own safety. Now was the time to draw the boundaries. He couldn't control the world.

Yet, Steve couldn't help feeling like a failure. He could only look at Benny, who returned his gaze with a shrug of his shoulders. At least he had gotten to know Benny better, Steve thought. Benny had been a true friend. Charlie had a friend after all.

"Leave him alone. Let him go. What more can we do?" Jang asked tersely.

Jang's words lifted Steve's spirits, but he still contemplated his options. He knew he still had time to chase Charlie, but his thoughts were cloudy, and this time there was no sunshine in sight. Steve had failed, and his promise to Jasmine was gone. Tomorrow would be worse than today.

"I'd better head on home," said Benny.

"No, don't be silly. Stay for a while. Come on in, man," said Steve.

This time it wasn't out of courtesy; Steve really wanted Benny to stay. Besides, he needed to find out where Charlie was going and what Benny knew of Charlie's life in Ashton. And to hear Benny's prediction of what Charlie might do tonight. He needed to gather more information. He needed to justify his failure.

"No, I should go, mang. It's getting late. I have to go to

work tomorrow."

Geez, Steve thought, Benny actually did have a job, unlike Charlie's other friends.

"I'm gonna go the other way so I won't pass your brother," said Benny, and, realizing what Steve was thinking, he quickly added, "Don't worry, mang, I won't pick him up."

In order to go home, Benny would normally take the same route Charlie was walking on. There was a detour, but he would have to take a left turn at the end of the driveway instead of the usual right turn. That was the way Benny meant to go.

Benny took a couple of steps towards his vehicle and turned to face Steve. "Yo, Steve. Really, mang, don't worry too much. He'll be alri..." He stopped his words suddenly and froze in his tracks. Steve snapped out of his daydream, raised his head to look at Benny, and instinctively turned in the direction Benny was looking. Charlie had reappeared on the front lawn and was walking quickly towards them. Before Steve could comprehend what was happening, Charlie passed them both and headed toward the front door of the house.

" I'm too fuckin' tired to walk. I'm going in," said Charlie as he slammed the door. Charlie was home!

CHAPTER TWENTY- ONE
coming home, part II

Steve could only look at Benny blankly. Jubilance filled his body for the second time today, this time stronger than the last. Steve could envision Jasmine seeing Charlie walk up the front stairs. She would be so happy, having all her family home at last. He felt a pang of emptiness. He closed his eyes to control his speeding heartbeat and swallowed a gulp of air. He did it. He had kept his promise to Jasmine. Just imagining her so happy made him squint his eyes and look up. He felt the summer breeze on his face as it gently caressed his skin and cooled his throbbing face. Even the night seemed to applaud him for a job well done. Something choked in his throat.

Steve didn't like to cry. At a young age, he learned that boys shouldn't cry. It was a sign of weakness, the elders told him. So young Steve refrained from crying. He wanted to be strong. He liked being strong. Yet, although he had no problem separating tears from physical pain, he couldn't do so when it came to emotional pain, especially when Jasmine cried. His sadness easily outweighed his reservation. Though he was aware that it made him seem like a crybaby, he knew that it was more than that. He cried because he saw how unfair and cruel this world could be to a person. He cried as one human being acknowledging the pain of another.

He also cried when he had to leave Jasmine to go back to college, usually while driving. It was because he knew that while a good life was waiting for him – mingling with affluent people who had good fortune smile on them since birth; dreaming with people who could afford to dream; being treated like an important person; learning anything and everything he wanted; partying on weekends with friends; feeling like a master of the universe; looking forward to tomorrow as another fun day – Jasmine would be working at the same menial task, assembling lighting fixtures, minute by minute, hour by hour, day by day, fighting to work even harder, fighting with Jang to let her work more, fighting with her jealous co-workers to give her more work. Every day she did the same. Steve felt guilty. The more he liked his college life, the more he felt guilty for what he left behind. He wished she could feel what he felt in school: the feeling of importance, the feeling of being educated, the feeling of being respected. He wished she could look forward to tomorrow as another day of fun. He wanted to give her that. He wanted to show her that. Yet he was the one who took from her – the cost of tuition, the living expenses, the books. Every time he left her, he felt he was betraying Jasmine and using her for her hard-earned money, while selfishly seeking an easy life for himself. It just didn't seem fair.

"Yo mang, I'm gonna go," said Benny. He sounded tired.

"You sure, man? Why don't you come in and have some food?"

"Nah, maybe next time. I should go home."

"Shit, Benny, my mom's gonna have a fit if you don't come in. Aren't you hungry? Let's go in and eat."

"Nah, that's all right, mang. I'm not really hungry. I should go."

As much as Steve wanted him to stay, Benny was right. It was family time. Steve never felt so close to any one of Charlie's friends. In fact, he never felt so close to any friend.

"All right. Hey, man, thanks for the help."

"Yeah. Later, mang."

Benny got in the vehicle, secured his seatbelt, started the vehicle, took a three-point turn, drove towards the end of the driveway and, to Steve's surprise, took the left turn, the detour. The thought of what might've happened still haunted Benny. Benny was aware that if Charlie hadn't come back, he might've never come back. Benny's gesture took the words right out of Steve's mind. He chuckled. If he were in Benny's position, he would've done the same. Benny was truly a friend.

Steve walked around the house, ready to open the back door, but stopped. Thirsty and dehydrated, he wanted to go in and maybe catch a glimpse of Jasmine's happy face, but something felt off. He couldn't go in. Not yet. He was confused. Was it because he didn't want to spoil Charlie's moment with their mother? His presence could indeed disturb this delicate moment. Charlie needed to be with Jasmine alone. But that wasn't the reason Steve hesitated.

It was because Steve felt like he didn't belong. He knew that was silly, but if ever he felt cheated by being born the second of three children, he felt it now. The middle child. The forgotten child. Jasmine had mentioned a few times that she loved Charlie the most because he was her first baby, and that she cared about Kimberly the most for being the last baby, and she trusted and respected Steve for who he was. 'Trusted and Respected' – as if he was the only one who had to *earn* his place in her heart. As if he wasn't born to belong to anyone. Maybe that was his destiny. He never thought about her comment until now.

The door seemed strangely unfamiliar, as if he was standing in front of someone else's house. Perhaps this was what Charlie felt. This was what Charlie had to fight with. But fate was on his side. Charlie was the rightful heir of the Lee family no matter what. Mother Nature had already decided on that long ago. According to Korean tradition, only the first-born truly carried the family lineage. What did Steve have to show for? Nothing! Not a thing! Who was he? What was he? Why was he lingering in someone else's doorway?

Steve's sense of belonging, his purpose, his place in the cosmos was diminishing with each second. He should've dismissed such a silly thought, but the overpowering sense of loneliness was too real to ignore. He felt he had borrowed his family for a short while, but now he had to give it back to its rightful owner. There was never any doubt who the real owner was; God had intended it that way. The true son of the family, the rightful owner, the carrier of the Lee family lineage was Charlie Lee. Steve was only a substitute, a benchwarmer, in case Charlie wasn't available. Steve couldn't help but envy Charlie, much like a peasant envying a prince. How delusional of him to have believed otherwise!

Just then, the door swung open. It was Charlie.

"Why aren't you coming in?" asked Charlie, his voice calm, as if nothing had happened. He seemed more relaxed and sure of himself now. Like an owner inviting a servant into his home.

"I'm just gonna hang out here for a minute. I'll go in later," said Steve, trying to disguise his feelings of inferiority.

Steve knew that showing some of those feelings was good for Charlie. Charlie needed confidence. Steve had managed them well during their adventures at the beach and at the police station. But he certainly hadn't planned on digging himself a hole this deep. He couldn't get out.

Charlie searched Steve's eyes. Steve looked back, but he soon looked away. This time the silence worked against him.

"Let's go in, bro," said Charlie.

"No, you go ahead. I just want to get some air out here."

"Come on. Mom's waiting for you."

"In a minute. I just want to stay here a bit."

"Are you all right?"

Steve paused. How could he explain what he was feeling to Charlie?

"Steve?"

Charlie walked towards Steve and hugged him. And he cried.

"I'm sorry Steve. I'm sorry. I've been nothing but bad to you. I'm sorry."

Charlie's voice shook from trying to talk and cry at the same time. He also spoke in Korean for the first time, reminding Steve of simpler times and how much they had changed since then.

All Steve could do was lightly hug Charlie back. He wasn't prepared for this. It was awkward. He felt grateful that Charlie opened up to him like this. That didn't happen very often. But then a slow undercurrent of defiance grew in him. Does he think I should forgive him now? he thought. He had done what he had to do, but forgiving Charlie was another story. There were too many things Charlie screwed up, too many headaches and too much heartache. There was no way he could forgive him just because he was crying and hugging him. No way! Although Steve hugged him back, Steve really wanted to let him go. He was tired of it all. Why was it always all about Charlie? What about Steve? What about his feelings? Didn't he matter to the family? Doesn't he matter at all?

Steve knew if there ever was a perfect time to cry, this was the time. The perfect time to bond, so that Charlie could feel forgiven. But that was precisely why Steve didn't want to. There was a limit to what he should do. He simply couldn't forgive Charlie. Steve's mission was to bring Charlie home. It was done, and that was all there was to it. After tonight, after Steve saw Charlie secured, he would plan on doing nothing with Charlie for a long time. Life is too short to be somebody's servant all the time.

Charlie seemed oblivious to Steve's feelings. He continued hugging him tightly, apologizing. He cried so hard he hiccupped, which echoed off the walls and porches of the house. Steve had to hug him tighter. He didn't want Charlie to feel like a fool in this one-way episode.

The faint smell of Charlie's sweatshirt brought back memories of the first time Steve was late for school. That was years ago. It was the last time Charlie ever hugged him so affectionately. Through the smell, Steve was almost hypnotized into traveling back in time. Everything came alive – the chilly wind, the autumn leaves, the hollow street, the loneliness, the fear, the anxiety, and, most of all, Charlie's love. Oh, how he cried for Charlie's safety that day when Charlie ran back to his homeroom and into the Tiger teacher's brutality after safely guiding Steve to his homeroom. Steve thought he would never see his big brother again. Instead of running to school to beat the clock, Charlie took his time, wiping young Steve's tears, crying with him, encouraging him not to quit. Charlie was by

Steve's side when he needed him the most, guiding Steve through his first real challenge.

Charlie was indeed tossed into desks by the Tiger teacher that day. The Tiger teacher wanted to make an example out of him in front of the entire class, especially because he was aware that Charlie was the natural leader of the students. Charlie was whipped on the butt twenty times with the monster paddle, which everyone called the Claw. But when young Steve asked him what happened, all Charlie said was, "Oh, nothing, just the usual shit." All Steve could think about was how good it was to see Charlie again. He worried all day for his safety. Steve was so thankful – Charlie Lee the guider, Charlie Lee the protector, Charlie Lee the hero.

And now Steve realized, Charlie Lee...the cold wind!

Everything he ever believed in lay in the smell of Charlie's sweatshirt: the love, the compassion, the identity, the sacrifice. It was what he was searching for all his life. How could he have forgotten? Charlie was always there for him. *Charlie was always there for him.* But now, Charlie needed him. The cold wind needed him.

Something twinged in Steve's nose, again and again. His eyes blurred and, though he tried to hold back, he knew it was hopeless. He had come home. Steve Lee belonged.

"I'm sorry I blamed you for everything. I'll try harder next time. I've never been a good big brother to you," said Charlie.

"Yes, you have," said Steve, gripping Charlie tighter, burying his face in his sweatshirt. And he cried.

CHAPTER TWENTY-TWO
water tears

Steve remained outside after Charlie went back into the house. Charlie urged Steve to go in with him, but he resisted. This time, he really wanted time to cool off. Jasmine wouldn't be ready for both of her sons coming home crying. He dusted himself more and fixed his hair. He wiped his face and stretched his arms. He rolled his neck and took a big breath. He stretched his jaw, shook his head and re-fixed his hair. But no matter what he did, he couldn't stop his tears from falling.

Big teardrops kept rolling off his face. He wasn't sad. In fact, he was happy, happy that everything turned out better than he had planned. Now, Steve felt free to cry to his heart's content. He wanted to let it all out, all that he had held back tonight. No one was around to witness his sappy drama. No one was around to tell him how a boy should or shouldn't behave or what he should or shouldn't do. Even if there was someone around, he didn't care this time. It felt good for him to cry. This was the first time in his life he cried for the sake of crying. And his tear factory certainly didn't let him down, supplying him with ample amounts. And they kept falling. Streams of tears rolled down his cheeks like an overflowing levee.

He was on such a roll that he had to find some excuses to cry. So he cried for Jasmine for her injustice; for Charlie for his shortcomings; for Jang for his sickness; for humanity for their sufferings. He felt light and his mind at ease. The tears weren't salty, nor did they carry any heat. In fact, they felt like water, washing over him, cleansing him. His water tears were tears of compassion, tears of sacrifice.

When does a boy become a man? This was a question Steve asked himself long ago. The answer seemed clear back then. In fact, he thought he knew for sure when he was in sixth grade. After having broken up one of Jasmine and Jang's particularly rough fights, Steve staggered outside the porch to calm down. He couldn't erase the vivid horror of Jasmine's face as she was being crushed by Jang's knee. Little seven-year-old Kimberly jumped in between them to stop them. The neighbors shut their windows to block out their noise, but no one called the police – oh, how Steve wished they did. Looking at the stars, he wondered when the world would come for him. When would he become a man so that he could right the wrong? There was so much he needed to repair. He could only pray for time to pass quickly. The designated date when he would become a man, he assumed, would be the day after his college graduation.

"I'll fix everything. I'll make everything good. I promise. I'll never forget this pain. When my world comes, when I graduate from college, everything will be different. Oh, please let time pass quicker. As you can see, I can't wait too long," Little Steve pleaded.

So he waited, while doing what he could to prepare for that impending moment. First, he made sure he didn't forget his pledge. He kept a thorough journal. Every time he felt he deviated from it, he reread all his journals. Second, he studied hard. When the time came, he would get a good job. If money were what his parents fought over, then they wouldn't need to fight anymore. They would have so much that they wouldn't know what to do with it. Even though he graduated from high school with many awards, he didn't bother to enjoy it because he had a higher purpose in mind – the final stretch into manhood: college.

A young warrior of ancient tribes becomes a man after killing a lion. The villagers would celebrate his metamorphosis by dancing around a bonfire, calling the ancestral spirits to join them, while the newly inducted warrior proudly displays his manhood by wearing the skin of the lion he killed. His purpose as a man is simple: to protect his tribe. So cool! Superboy becomes Superman after he discovers who he really is, where he comes from, and what his purpose on earth is. He celebrates by flying into the sunset with a distinctive sparkle in his eyes, wearing a red cape and bearing the insignia "S" on his chest. His purpose as a man is simple: to protect society in the true American Way. So, so cool!

For Steve, he would receive the enlightenment on the day of his college graduation. His family would celebrate the day with rice wine, praising his black robe and golden tassel. With all his education, all his knowledge, and all his determination, he would set forth into the new world with the iron strength he garnered. His purpose would be simple: to do what was right for his family. It would be so cool. But as he neared his graduation date, he became more apprehensive than excited. He didn't know how it was going to happen or if it would happen at all. And, on the day of graduation, instead of feeling manly, he felt more confused than ever before. It seemed like the more he knew, the more he realized how much he didn't know. The world was too big to care about his supposed metamorphosis. Nothing changed. He still felt like a scared boy, maybe even more so than before, and the problems of his family didn't go away. In fact, they increased. So, he asked again: When does a boy become a man in this society?

Jasmine once told him a boy becomes a man after he serves his country in the military. She married Jang soon after he finished serving his three years of mandatory military service. But could anyone blame Steve if he didn't believe Jang didn't fulfill all of his manly duties? Does a boy become a man after he makes love for the first time? After all, making love was grown-up stuff. Procreation is the scientific explanation for the meaning of life. Or is it when a boy gets married? Some people have said a boy becomes a man after he holds his baby in his arms for the first time. But, to Steve, none of this seemed like the definite answer. Some of Steve's classmates were having sex and having babies when they were in high school. Some got married; some because they had babies. No one could possibly think that they were men.

In the end, Steve concluded that maybe being a man was all an act, that there was no clear line to define manhood, that everyone only pretended. Maybe being a man is about what you wear, how you talk, or how you act, but not about how you feel, he thought. If you pretend it long enough maybe everyone will buy into it, including yourself. Maybe age and stature – when they change to father, mister, doctor, sir, professor, or whatever – are the best elements to disguise yourself from the scared boy inside you. You might then think you've become a man, but what you really do is hide the scared boy. By then, you wouldn't be able to reveal your true self even if you wanted to because no one else would want you to. Revealing the scared little boy inside you could mean that you played them for suckers. Or even worse, it could persuade them to reveal theirs. So you decide to continue to make believe and do things that are defined by your society to be manly – what your scared boy thinks is manly – like make money, make power, make love, and make babies. Maybe the so-called man's ambition is born out of fear of the scared boy's self-worth. Maybe being a man in this world is only about an ongoing charade of a scared little boy hiding himself from the truth, the truth being that no one really knows the line that defines manhood.

But now, Steve realized he was wrong to think that. There was a clear line to define manhood, and that every boy must search his own. Steve's decision to bring Charlie home didn't happen randomly. That was Steve's line. It carried a greater purpose, to let him manifest all that he prepared to find what he was seeking. And he conquered it. There was a different kind of lion he killed today, the beast's skin wrapping his comforting soul. Steve wasn't afraid anymore. He knew his purpose in life, the purpose of his existence. Tomorrow, and the tomorrow after that, he would tackle his role head on. There will be no more doubts. However small he might be in this world, he was one of the protectors of the greatest treasure known to it: love. Steve's tears were his celebration. From the moment water tears rolled over his eyes, Steve knew he crossed the line into manhood. The world finally came for him.

ABOUT THE AUTHOR

Han D. Cho graduated from Cornell University in 1989, and has since taught martial arts to thousands of students in his community and at his alma mater, capturing a record 21 ECTC championship titles. Many of his students have gone on to become national level players, coaches, and masters. In 2015, he was promoted to the rank of 9th Dan, the highest in the martial art that he teaches. He lives with his wife, Alice, with whom he shares the joys of raising their caring daughter and curious son.

Made in the USA
Charleston, SC
06 December 2016